Jo Frost is one of the UK's most trusted, leading childcare and parental guidance experts. As the the most recognisable face of parenting on television, Jo's books and TV projects have received huge international acclaim and are seen and written in many languages throughout the world. Her most recent book, *Jo Frost's Confident Toddler Care*, was a *Sunday Times* Number 1 bestseller.

For further information on Jo and her work, please visit: www.jofrost.com and follow her on Twitter @ Jo_Frost.

I dedicate this book to John Lloyd.

A loving father and husband who inspired me and is indeed responsible for planting the seed, making the invisible visible, and sharing my knowledge via the beauty of books. With much gratitude I thank you.

Love,

JoJo xx

Jo Frost's
Toddler SOS

Practical Solutions for the
Challenging Toddler Years

Jo Frost

This edition first published in Great Britain in 2013 by
Orion Books
an imprint of the Orion Publishing Group Ltd
Orion House, 5 Upper St Martin's Lane,
London WC2H 9EA
An Hachette UK Company

1 3 5 7 9 10 8 6 4 2

A CIP catalogue record for this book is available
from the British Library.

ISBN: 978 0 7528 9864 3

Printed and bound in China

The Orion Publishing Group's policy is to use papers that are natural,
renewable and recyclable and made from wood grown in sustainable
forests. The logging and manufacturing processes are expected to
conform to the environmental regulations of the country of origin.

Note: *All children are unique and this book is not intended to be a substitute
for the advice of your doctor or health visitor who should be consulted on
toddler matters, especially when a child shows any sign of illness or unusual
behaviour. Neither the publisher nor the author accepts any legal responsibility
for any personal injury or other damage or loss arising from the use or
misuse of the information and advice in this book.*

Illustrations by Helen Flook

Every effort has been made to fulfil requirements with regard to
reproducing copyright material. The author and publisher will be
glad to rectify any omissions at the earliest opportunity.

www.orionbooks.co.uk

Contents

A Special Little Note From Me

Thank you Orion, for your dedicated, attentive and hard working team who continue to believe and support my brand and in return have helped so many families and that's what counts!

Mary Jane Ryan, how lucky am I? You are one of the hardest working women I know! Thank you for yet again helping me deliver a book I'm very proud of.

Daniel Pangbourne, there truly is no one who can photograph children like you. Thank you!

To Helen Flook: your adorable artwork has complemented this book and my others so, so well, thank you!

To the darling little cherubs on the cover of this book who made the day so much fun: Isabella, Flora and Jake, thank you and your wonderful parents who made it happen.

Dr Mark Furman, a big thank you for your time and support, it is very much appreciated.

Cynthia Ross, thank you for all of your hard work helping to get this book done.

Jennie Lyons, a special thank you for being my 24/7 go-to book researcher and of course for being the wonderful friend that you are in my life!

To my family and closest friends who continue to uplift me every day: I love you all xoxoxo

Introduction

As your child moves through the toddler years, you might find yourself asking similar questions to those of the parents in this book: 'How can I get my daughter to play nicely with others?', 'Why did my son pull his sister's hair?', 'My child won't poo in the potty, what can I do to help her?', or 'Why, why, why won't he stay in bed?' The toddler years are full of questions for parents, just as they are for toddlers.

That's because, when the toddler phase arrives, it can seem like you've got a whole new person on your hands. Well the truth is, in many ways, you have. When babies become toddlers, they certainly do change. They become little people who express themselves in lots of different ways. Hello, Mum, hello Daddy! Let me introduce you to your child.

Sometimes what that child does is delightful; at other times it's frustrating or upsetting. Tantrums and meltdowns, biting, throwing, hitting, screaming, not listening . . . The toddler years can be very challenging for parents. That's because there are three main ways a newly mobile toddler typically expresses himself: hitting himself (or head-butting walls, for example), hitting others (as well as biting, nipping, pulling hair), and/or doing 'naughty' things like putting toast in the DVD player. I call the latter exploration – trying things that seem fun because they're new. None of these behaviours are fun to deal with in the moment.

As your child goes from ages one to five, you will need to cultivate five qualities above all others: patience, persistence, follow-through, consistency and repetition. These attitudes are what toddlers need from you above all else. That's because toddlers are not built with a chip that allows them to understand something the first time you say it. They are not built knowing how to be

patient. They are not built knowing how to wait, how to queue, how to reason
. . . They are not built knowing what's important to you. And the reason why
is because our toddlers are not robots! Everything your toddler needs to learn
comes from *you,* his parent, his child-minder, his grandparents, his immediate
family.

Children's brains are like blank canvases and we paint the picture. We do
that not only by teaching, but through leading by example, by being great role
models and exhibiting the behaviour that we want to see. Children are not
built knowing how to respect another child or a parent. They are taught this
by the honour and the grace and the respect that we give them. And then that
behaviour is modelled back. It's like when you stroke your child's hair and give
her lots of cuddles and you pat her back when she's hurt herself, and then later
she gives you a massage or a pat on the back. She models your behaviour.

Raising a toddler also requires commitment and willingness. It's not like
you're taking a three-day intensive course in first aid at St John's Ambulance and
now you know it. Every day's an ongoing challenge. The pay-off is that you will

be making life more pleasant in the long run and eliminating bigger problems later. That's because, as you go about your daily life with this little person, you are setting the foundation for self-control, the ability to listen to and follow directions, and the beginning of responsibility and independence. Fortunately the rewards of these years are wonderful – this is also the time when kids say the cutest, funniest things and the pride on their faces when they've mastered something new is priceless. And the ultimate pay-off for all your work is huge: you are helping shape a unique, one-of-a-kind human being into a healthy, happy adult.

But that doesn't make any given moment easy. Because these years can be so demanding, a lot of my work has been focused on helping parents navigate this time of life. That's why I was so happy to write *Confident Toddler Care* last year and why I am so pleased to offer you *Toddler SOS* now. While *Confident Toddler Care* is an encyclopedia of my wisdom on raising toddlers, *Toddler SOS* is that wisdom applied to questions parents have emailed, tweeted, posted online, asked me on the street – wherever I am in the public eye – about the real concerns they have as they go about their day with their toddler: Why isn't the Naughty Step working? How can I get him to bed on time? Why is she playing with her wee and what can I do about it? These and over one hundred of your most pressing questions are covered in this book.

If you've watched my TV shows and read my other books, you may be very familiar with some of the techniques I offer. I suggest them because they work – when you do them with patience, persistence, follow-through, consistency and repetition. However, some people have come up to me and said certain techniques don't work. When I ask them to describe the steps, they can't, which tells me they're not following them exactly. This book addresses that as well. It is my hope that in reading how I apply my techniques in specific situations, you can learn how to use them effectively in your unique circumstances.

If you are reading this sentence now, you've had the foresight to learn from the questions other parents are asking and you understand that raising your child is your responsibility. It makes sense, doesn't it? We can't blame the school for why our child isn't learning when we get back reports that he won't sit down for five minutes. We can't blame the supermarkets for selling high-processed salty and sugary foods when we buy them and give them to our children. I want to help turn the conversation around so parents say, I am responsible for my son getting good reports at school because I taught him the appropriate life skills. I am responsible for my child being healthy because of the choices I make.

I am responsible for my daughter playing happily with friends because I taught her how.

I'm not saying it is easy for parents in a society with so many pressures and with so many support systems shutting down and so much conflicting information being given. Regardless, common sense is common sense and we can make sure we offer our young ones the fundamentals using our common sense. Don't wait until she is five years old and a challenging child. You should start instilling good values, proper behaviour and respect for others from the earliest time your toddler can understand. This will make your job as a parent so much more enjoyable, and your child so much nicer to have around.

Come on, let's be real. Recently, I saw a mum with her family in a hotel. She had four young children eating lunch in the restaurant and they were all sitting around the table together, with napkins on their laps, having a wonderful conversation with each other and behaving beautifully. It was refreshing to see – I gave her a big smile of acknowledgement. This was clearly a mother who understood the importance of what she had to instil and now all of them were reaping the benefits. No, this mum wasn't a Disneyland mum. She was a mum who understood clearly what was important to her in raising her children.

These days, where consumerism is king and we all find ourselves increasingly time-poor, it's too easy to think you're showing your child how much you love her by giving her things she wants all the time. But material items can't replace giving your child the time and attention she needs. Even if you only get two hours a day with your child, try to make sure those hours are quality time for you and her. Believe me, your child will value this much more than anything you could buy her.

It takes time and effort to be a mum or dad. You can't clock in and out, and it doesn't come instantly for some. Your relationship with your child takes time to grow – and you need to grow as well. Sometimes there are no instant fixes. Bear in mind that it will take time to find solutions to your parenting dilemmas and stick with your decisions. It's my hope that the answers you find here in this book will help you with your choices and give you the stamina to see those choices through. One of the key mistakes parents make with toddlers is a lack of consistency. They try something that takes time and they lose patience with the technique and say it doesn't work. It is my hope that this book helps you stay the course, that it encourages and motivates you to implement the change.

In saying that, as you go through these years, please don't be too hard on yourself when you slip up. When you're wrong, just tell yourself you're learning from your mistakes and do it differently next time. This creates healthy, positive behaviours for you and sets a healthy, positive example for your child. And that's the very best lesson you can offer your family.

Come on, the pages await you.

Jo
xxxx

1

Bonding

Every parent has heard about the importance of bonding. But what does that really mean? If something bonds, it sticks together, and if it's tight, it can't be broken. When you bond with your child, you create a trusting and open relationship that has loving feelings and healthy communication, and offers your child a sense of security, the feeling that you're there for her, full stop. Creating and maintaining a strong, loving relationship with your child is one of the key tasks of parenthood. It is the foundation for all of the relationships in her life.

A bond with your child is formed from the natural, loving feelings you each have, along with the time, attention and nurturing you offer throughout her growing up. It develops out of experiences you create that allow your relationship to become more intimate. When you carve out the time to enjoy experiences together, to listen to one another, to talk about different things and to have fun, you develop and strengthen the bonds between you. We all remember enjoyable experiences we've had with other people. We remember because those experiences are attached to emotion. If we *have* a really good experience and feel very happy in that experience and we enjoy it, the brain remembers it. And we feel closer to the person we were with.

The toddler years can raise many questions about this connection: how much time is enough? How do I make sure I'm doing it right? Is quality really more important than quantity? Working mums in particular worry about this. Then there is the issue of toddlers favouring one parent over the other. Or how to deal with a toddler bonding with a parent who does not live with her. I hope the answers I provide in this section help you and your partner to deepen your emotional connection with your toddler and reduce any sense of guilt.

IN THIS CHAPTER

- ◆ **Carving out quality time**
- ◆ **Working parents and bonding**
- ◆ **Easy fun activities to do with your child**
- ◆ **Toddler preferring one parent over another**
- ◆ **Creating quality story-telling time**
- ◆ **Making time for each child when you have siblings or multiples**
- ◆ **Helping your toddler bond with a non-custodial parent**

Quality Time?

Q I am a working mother of two young toddlers who suffers from guilt over not being with them all day. I hear so much about how it's not the amount of time we spend with our kids, but the quality of the time. How do I make sure the time I do spend is 'quality'?

A Quality time is time when you interact with your child on a one-to-one basis or together with all your children when they have your full attention. It is uninterrupted and undistracted. You're not cooking with one eye and looking at what they are doing with the other, saying, 'That's great, honey.' Quality time allows you to connect with your children, to get to know them better, to develop and deepen your relationship. Rather than feel guilty about working, I would encourage you to become strong in your intention to set aside time each day to engage fully with your children. That means resisting picking up the phone, dealing with the emails and tidying the house for some period of time so that you can focus exclusively on them.

Parents always ask me how much time is enough. My emphasis would be more on making sure you are undistracted during the time you spend with them rather than worrying about how long you spend with them. Trying for an hour or two a day can feel so overwhelming that you don't do it at all. I'd rather you take a bite-size amount than a big mouthful. It is better to be consistent and give your kids the same time every day than to be sporadic with the time that you spend with them. I would suggest carving out half an hour a day during the weekdays. That gives you time to start a project, enjoy it, and then wrap it up nicely.

Parents often struggle over what to do to bond with their child. With toddlers, it's all about playing. Let your hair down, be silly and have fun, whether that is rolling around on the floor, racing in the garden, colouring together, or playing Snakes and Ladders. You may find yourself becoming bored with playing the same games over and over. But toddlers love repetition because it helps them learn.

You don't need to spend money on fancy toys. It's about recognising what resources are around you. I used to play memory games with my charges by collecting a few knick-knacks from around the house and putting them on a tray, then taking something away and seeing if they can figure out what is missing. Or I've taken used paper and balled it up to throw in a bucket to see if we can get it in. It really doesn't matter what you do if you are able to have fun.

And if you can help your children become more co-ordinated because you're being physically active with them, even better.

You and your child can also experience quality time during the bed-time routine. Bathing, reading a bed-time story, snuggling together – these are all things that create lasting memories and bonds, as well as improving their literacy and social skills tremendously.

Weekends are great for activities that take more time than you have during the weekdays. Here is where you and your partner can have a chance to have one-on-one time with each child, as well as enjoy family time together. These activities don't have to be fancy or expensive. Just being together is what matters, especially to your little ones, so enjoy. (See box opposite for ideas.)

Working Mother Worrying about Bond

Q *I am a single mum of an 18-month son and have to work two jobs to keep us afloat. I feel I am short-changing my son while trying to make a living for us. My parents help me with childcare and he adores them. In fact, it feels like he would rather be with them than me. Any suggestions on how to keep from losing a precious bond with my son?*

A You are being a very responsible parent, earning a living as best you can – GOOD FOR YOU! It's not always easy, striving for balance between work and family. Let's face it, millions of families are doing this every day, especially in this economic climate. Try not to be so hard on yourself, give yourself a little break here. I really don't think for one minute your son would rather be without his mother. I just think you're worrying that that just might be the case because you feel guilty about working so much. Obviously your son loves his grandparents and it's great he is able to bond with them, but being with his mother is no comparison and nothing can change that.

Make sure that you spend solo quality time with your son when you are not working. (See my suggestions in the previous question.) Interacting with him mentally, emotionally and physically will develop the special connection between you and both of you will feel a lot happier. You are what he wants and needs – an attentive and nurturing mother. So please release yourself of the guilt you are carrying, keep positive and enjoy every minute you spend together.

FREE FUN ACTIVITIES WITH TODDLERS

Inside

◆ **Blowing bubbles**

◆ **Safari Time:** make animal masks and crawl around the living room as your favourite animal

◆ **Egg-decorating**

◆ **Playing in the sink with dishwashing liquid and plastic containers**

◆ **Pirates and Princesses:** making forts and castles out of furniture

◆ **Dress up** – let them clomp around the house in your shoes

◆ **Mini world:** Wendy houses and/or make-believe shops

◆ **Feet- and hand-painting using finger-paints**

◆ **Queen's Tea Party:** make a crown and create a tea party in a special place

◆ **Dancing and playing musical instruments**

Outside

◆ **Collecting pebbles to paint them at home**

◆ **Walks in garden centres or wetlands, collecting leaves to do rubbings**

◆ **Play times at church halls**

◆ **Rolling down hills**

◆ **Library story-telling time**

◆ **Visiting castles (kids are free) and farms**

◆ **Going to a free-entry museum**

◆ **Feeding the ducks at the park**

◆ **Making sandcastles at the beach**

Is My Working Causing Her Problems?

Q My 18-month-old is starting to have tantrums and be even clingier than when she was younger. I'm afraid this is happening because I work full-time and she has to go to a child-minder. Is she acting like this because I am not with her all day?

A It is very common for many mothers to feel the way you do. Working mothers blame themselves for practically everything because emotionally they feel torn between having to work and wanting to be at home raising their kids. The reason why your 18-month-old is more clingy than when she was younger is because she is at the developmental stage when children go through separation anxiety.

Every toddler tests boundaries and pushes to control situations regardless of whether her mother is a stay-at-home or one who works. These are all normal toddler behaviours. Please read this book as well as *Confident Toddler Care* so that you will see how familiar your toddler's behaviour is.

If you continue feeling so guilty, you may respond inappropriately when she acts out or pushes the boundaries you have set for her. Also guilty mums make excuses for their children's naughty behaviour, which can then lead to becoming over-indulgent. A working parent's over-indulgence often also takes the form of giving a child too many material things, which can result in a sense of entitlement which leads to selfishness and greed.

Here is what you can do. When you come home make sure to do something with her that she really loves doing. Talk to her when you are tucking her into bed about the fun things that you will do when you come home from work tomorrow and the things you will do when Mummy is not at work on the weekends.

On a personal note, it will help you to get a rundown every day from the child-minder on what your daughter did and enjoyed that day. That way you will feel more a part of her life when you are at work.

Doesn't Want Daddy

Q *My three-year-old daughter is a Mama's girl. She wants me to do everything with her and refuses to co-operate when my husband tries to get her ready in the morning, give her a bath or put her to bed. I feel badly for my husband – I can only imagine how it makes him feel when she screams for me – but I confess I give in to keep the peace.*

A With your last sentence, you're acknowledging that you already know you're making it worse. Your daughter has found a very effective way to get exactly what she wants. She screams, you give in, and if you continue to do that, things will never change.

Toddlers can get fixated on one parent, especially if they spend more time with one than the other. But you can encourage a healthy relationship with her father as well. Begin by having you and your husband take turns doing the evening routine. And stick to the schedule no matter how your daughter reacts!

When it's your husband's evening, explain to your daughter that tonight is Daddy's turn and that it is yours tomorrow and that while Daddy is giving her a bath and the two of you are having fun, Mummy is going to be getting other things done. At first, she'll scream because that's worked in the past. Your husband will need to stay calm and you will need to resist stepping in no matter how worked up she gets. If it's hard for you to listen to her cries, try being away for an hour at her bed time, at least the first few times. Perhaps you could speak to a friend on the phone and be distracted by catching up with them. Or set aside a chore that needs to get done so that you can focus on that. As your daughter starts to get used to the idea of her parents taking turns, the tantrums will lessen. The most important thing is to stay on course. You can also alternate the morning routine if that works for you both.

It's equally important that Dad and daughter spend quality time together as this allows their bond to grow too, and enables your husband to become more emotionally attached. Playing a special game that is labelled 'their game' and creating a 'Daddy and Me Time' will have her eagerly looking forward to spending time with him. The most important issue here is your partner knowing that his daughter's rejection is not personal but more a case of what she is used to.

Not Enjoying My Child

I'm a full-time mother. I spend lots of the day doing chores and lots of my time alone with my two-year-old. She's becoming increasingly naughty, she screams when I ask her to eat or get dressed or if I try to brush her teeth. Everything is a battle. I'm so worried I don't actually like my own child. I can't wait until bed time every day. What can I do?

When parents are challenged by their children's misbehaviour, it can feel ever so personal. And when parents have difficult challenges with their children, they tend not to like the day-to-day experience of parenthood. This can strain the relationship between you, which makes it even more difficult to bond with your child.

That's why the first and foremost issue here is to create a routine that is structured enough to allow you to do household chores and daily activities with your child and is flexible enough to allow her to make choices in certain areas of her life.

Look at the *tone* with which you run your day. If your attitude is very military, then your child is going to feel like you're a sergeant-major and you're dictating: 'Get up! Eat! Get dressed! Let's go!' If you have such an attitude, you're *absolutely* going to meet resistance. Because within a routine that a parent carves out for her child, balancing meeting her needs and the chores that must be done, it needs to feel like you're encouraging your child to experience all that is out there for her. Rather than, 'We *have* to do this!' it should be, 'Let's do this because it's going to be a really fun experience.' I don't think that your two-year-old is really feeling that from you.

Compromise where you *can*, so that not everything is a battle with your child. Certain things, like brushing teeth, are necessary. But change where you do it. Maybe she brushes her teeth in the bath. Maybe she brushes them when she gets out of the bath. Give her choices. Instead of 'There are the clothes you're wearing', ask her 'Which of these three T-shirts do you want to wear?' What she's fighting you for right now is some independence, which s natural and normal for toddlers. In her mind, she's thinking, 'I want to try this. I see my parents do it and I want to do it too!' Let her dress herself, even if it takes longer and she doesn't do it perfectly. Let her pour the cereal even if a bit spills.

If you can give her more choice and more opportunities to do things herself, I don't think you'll have as many battles. And if you're not battling, you'll be able to enjoy doing things together. And from that, the bonding will grow.

Won't Sit Still to Read

Q *I'm a dad who works all day and loves the bed-time routine I do with my daughter. But she just won't sit and read with me. I know reading is an important part of her development and I feel like I'm failing here. How do I make the situation better?*

A Congratulations – you understand that it is absolutely crucial that you read to your child. It will help her speech, vocabulary and literacy skills. I wholeheartedly encourage parents to read to their child every night.

I don't think there is one parent who hasn't experienced the situation you're describing. You have it in your mind that you're going to have a wonderful, bonding story time where everything is quiet, and your toddler is running around like Speedy Gonzales. That's because toddlers don't have long attention spans. That's why they may get up or be distracted by something in the room. But it doesn't mean that they're not listening. Here's how you tell: a child who's still listening is not fully engaging in something else. She may move around a bit, but she comes back to you. She'll look at the pictures. I think that is okay. That's different from being defiant and misbehaving, which must be dealt with.

As your child gets older, her attention span will grow. Here's what you can do now to help her attention span, as well as make story time a wonderful experience for you both:

◆ **Set up the expectation with your daughter that when we get out of the bath and we put our pyjamas on we're going to do some reading.**

◆ **Create as much of a distraction-free environment as possible. Don't read next to the squeaky push and pull toys, for instance.**

◆ **Allow her to participate in choosing the books, and how many times the story is going to be read. Toddlers love repetition – it's how they learn.**

- **Read in an animated and energetic tone. Give a different voice to each character. This really helps draw your child in and become engaged. (Right now, I bet you are thinking: 'Really Jo? When I've just done a whole day at work and I'm feeling tired, you're asking me to put on a performance?' Yes. I am asking you to find that reserve in your tank and pull it out because you want to spend quality bonding time with your child.)**

- **Ask her to turn the pages.**

- **If she begins to wander away, ask questions about what you're reading to bring her back to the story.**

- **If she is distracted by wanting to play with something else, remove it so that the sole attraction is the book.**

- **If she starts running around and getting into something else, say, 'Daddy's reading you a story. I need you to stay close and listen.' Then ask her something about the story: 'What is the pig going to do next? Come here and we'll find out!'**

Parents ask me if you ever put the book away and put your child to bed without a story if she is not listening. I think it depends on the circumstances. If your child is going through a phase right now where she's misbehaving and you haven't got that under wraps, then *every* night you're going to be closing that book. That's not the right thing to do because your child's not going to learn. Instead, you have to nip that behaviour in the bud with a warning and a consequence and then go back to the book so that your child will learn to sit down and become engaged in the story. If, however, you've been reading together for a while and every now and then your child becomes distracted, then you've got leverage to say, 'Right, no story tonight then!' She'll soon realise she's missing out on something because it's part of her routine and she will want it back.

Making Time for the Youngest

Q *I am a mother of five kids. How do I make time for my youngest, who is two years old? I feel like he is always being dragged along with everything I have to get done in the day.*

Yes, five kids are certainly a handful, to say the least. But I have to say, I'm encouraged that you recognise that your youngest may need more attention. Really, this is all about routine. When you've got five kids, you cannot afford *not* to run a tight ship. A routine allows you to put things in place that are very important for them and gives you sanity at the same time. The more you can become efficient about a routine, the more you can meet each child's needs with respect to establishing healthy meal times, having bed-time routines that enable a wind-down period and sleep, creating times for the children to bond with one another, and have one-on-one time with you. With your two-year-old, I would think about finding one-on-one time in the mornings while the other children are at school to do the early learning activities that are so necessary for his development. This focused attention is one of the best things you can give him.

EARLY LEARNING ACTIVITIES

- Doing puzzles
- Building blocks, Lego and construction sets
- Threading beads
- Colouring and finger-painting
- Playing matching games like colour-matching and animals' tops and tails
- Throwing and catching a ball
- Throwing bean bags into the washing basket
- Doing shape sorters

Individual Time for Triplets

I am a father of triplets. I don't get to see them much during the week. They all want my time at the same time during the weekends. How do I make them all feel special and loved?

Many parents who have multiples want to know how to make each of their children feel special and loved. It's certainly not what we say, but what we do with them. As somebody who works during the week, your weekends are precious. This is when you get to create family time, when you all do things together. At the same time, it's equally important to develop your relationship with each child individually. Because even though they're dealt with as a unit – eating at the same time, sleeping at the same time, off to the park at the same time – they each have their own personalities and spirits. One-on-one time is not only important for your kids, but also for you. It allows you to get to know each one better and become closer.

To make sure each one has individual attention, set up two with something to do while you're having half an hour with one. Then switch to the next. You don't necessarily have to be outside the house to do this. Let them know that you are going to spend time with each in turn. As long as you follow through, they will accept it.

Bonding with Out-of-Town Dad

I'm a single mum who wants to help my 14-month-old daughter bond with her dad when he comes to visit. She only gets to see him a few times a year since he lives out of the country. When he does visit, he expects there to be an instant physical bond. I have tried giving him advice many times (let her warm up to you first, etc.), but he doesn't listen. She cries almost every time he takes her from me. She is very clingy when he is in town and will rarely play if he is in the room. I have to bite my lip and leave the room since he won't give in to her crying for Mummy. It's tough, but I tell myself it is only for a few days.

He is very stubborn and short-tempered. He would never strike either of us, but if I am not careful he may not talk to us. This has happened a couple of times over very little things. He has a good heart and I want him in our daughter's life. I'm just worried that she may grow up not liking him.

I can see why you would feel so anxious. The distance can make situations feel more heightened. However, let's get down to your question. At 14 months old, all children go through a stage of clinginess regardless of whether they see their father more often than not. Your email relays that you are not exactly elated around your ex's company, and that will also make your daughter sense this edginess. That is because you know that he can be short-tempered, so when you hand over your daughter you feel panicked because you hope he is going to be fair to the child you have together. Your daughter also feels panicked because she feels her father's impatience. You have shown me that there is a fear of him not talking to you both again and it leads me to question if there is still hostility in your relationship even though there is no commitment any more. I urge you both to sit down and smoothe out any remaining issues so that you can both understand that this is about the child you have together.

Here are my suggestions for helping your toddler feel more connected to the parent she sees infrequently:

- Have him call her on the phone regularly. It may work more easily if it is a regular time, for example, after bath time. Hearing his voice or Skyping is a way of communicating and connecting.

- Having him send photos with letters allows you to convey to your child her parents' feelings and pointing to the photo affirms that: 'That's Daddy and he misses you very much.'

- When they spend time together, have him take photos of them together having fun so they can be framed and put in the bedroom to remind her of the good times they share.

- Before the other parent comes to collect, remind your child this is happening so that when you do hand her over, you feel okay about it and your child will be reassured because you are.

- If you have an amicable relationship and are both committed to your children, even if not to one another, grab 15 minutes together to catch up on what your child has been up to so that the child can see that there is healthy conversation between you. It helps to heal the new family dynamic.

- Use this opportunity to have some down time and do something nice for yourself, whether it is taking a long bath, flicking through magazines with a cup of coffee or talking to your friends. It is important that you recharge your batteries.

- Last but not least, when your child is dropped back home obviously you can convey you have missed your child. Make sure that you also convey that you hope that they had lots of good time together and that Mummy was busy catching up on things and that was good for her while you were having fun.

IN CHAPTER 2

- ◆ How to do the Naughty Step properly
- ◆ What age you should start using the Naughty Step
- ◆ What behaviour is not appropriate for the Naughty Step and what to do instead
- ◆ Getting spouses and carers on the same discipline page
- ◆ My view on smacking
- ◆ Disciplining multiples

2

Discipline

It is the parents' responsibility to make sure that their children know how to behave respectfully towards other human beings and understand how their behaviour affects others. Children are not born knowing these things. That's why, from the age of 18 months two years onwards, children need to be taught right from wrong – what is acceptable behaviour and what isn't. And it is parents who are the primary regulators and teachers of proper behaviour to children. You do this by setting clear boundaries and warnings, and then providing consequences if the boundaries aren't followed.

That's what discipline is – giving a consequence that allows a child to sit down and think about his behaviour so that he becomes more conscious as he grows older of what's morally right. (That's one of the reasons I am against smacking. It curbs behaviour from pain, not from learning. It doesn't help a child reflect on his behaviour and learn to make better choices. Instead, it teaches him that when you get angry and you don't like something, it's okay to hit.)

If parents don't put proper rules and consequences in place when a child is young, what we start to see is human behaviour become all out of sorts. A child's ability to learn is lessened because he won't listen to teachers and is not able to sit still. His ability to have healthy relationships is hindered because he feels he can dominate and bully and be verbally unkind. And the older he gets, the more his behaviour becomes hardwired and the more difficult to change.

If, however, parents understand the importance of creating boundaries and disciplining when those boundaries are crossed, then they end up raising a child who is consciously aware of his behaviour and its impact on others. He takes responsibility for his behaviour. He has healthy relationships with friends and family and is able to bring out his full potential academically.

To be truly effective, discipline must be consistent. You can't one day discipline your child because she's hurt another toddler and turn a blind eye to the same thing another day or in another situation. Because it doesn't teach her that we're serious about the situation or that it's important to us.

As anyone who's ever seen me in action on TV, read my books or heard me talk about parenting will know, I am a firm believer in implementing consistent discipline when toddlers act up. There are several effective techniques I teach parents to shape better behaviour from their children. They each allow you to teach your children *in the moment* what was wrong with what they did. The most famous is the Naughty Step and all its variations – Naughty Chair, Naughty Spot, Naughty Mat, Naughty Circle. It gives a child the space to sit and then be told why she's had to sit there. Over time, this repetitive action soaks in and she understands what is expected of her so that when she becomes older and less impulsive, she can curb her own behaviour.

While the Naughty Step technique is straightforward, parents have many questions about it: When is it not appropriate? At what age to start it? Why isn't it working? When should you do something else? What if you and your partner disagree about it? This section will answer those questions.

I know from years of first-hand experience that when a technique is not working, it's because parents are ignoring a crucial step or failing to follow through. Hopefully, in these pages you'll gain the knowledge you need to make this technique work for you. It is amazing to me how many parents that I have visited say, 'This isn't working!' and when I watch them do it they have missed step two or three. Or they find excuses for why they cannot do it. This chapter can help.

How to Implement the Naughty Chair

Q *Can you explain exactly how to use the Naughty Chair? We have begun using it on our three-year-old son for about one and a half months and it does not seem to be working. We put him in the chair (which is located in our family room), we tell him what he did wrong, and have him sit there for three minutes. Most of the time he cries and begs to get up or he slides out of the chair. After the time is up, he does the same behaviour again and back in the Naughty Chair he goes.*

A The Naughty Chair (Step, Mat, Circle, etc.) technique is all about the steps you take and understanding how those steps work towards a productive goal. See the box on pages 26–27 for a step-by-step explanation and be sure not to miss any steps. Part of what I see you are not doing is giving a warning. It's important to give your child the warning in an authoritative voice and explain what you want to stop: 'If you hit your sister again, you will go to the Naughty Chair.'

Ignore the crying and begging. If you have chosen to use a Chair and he sits next to it instead of on it, then as long as he isn't moving from that space he's getting discipline. Once his three-minute time out is over, make sure you reinforce what he did wrong when you go back to talk to him: 'You hit your sister and that's not okay because that hurt her and that is naughty behaviour.' You want to make sure learning is happening. If he does it again, start over. He is testing to see if you really mean it. Remember, *you* hold the authority, not the chair.

If you find you are repeating this technique every five minutes, then think about whether you are setting unrealistic expectations for your child. Look to see why the hitting is happening. Perhaps you need to work on sharing with siblings. The Naughty Chair will not teach that, you have to.

Throwing the Naughty Chair

Q *What do I do when my child throws the chair he's supposed to be sitting on?*

A If you've chosen to use a Naughty Chair and your child, in rage, throws the chair, then you know that you're dealing with a child who is extremely angry because you've taken away his control and laid down the law. I would remove the chair and use a Naughty Spot instead. Just pick a place where he must stay. Make sure there is nothing around the spot that he can throw. Because if he's still angry, he's going to throw whatever is at hand to try to get your attention so you won't follow through. If he moves away from the spot, place him back and reset the timer. But make sure that you have no communication with him.

Follow Through!

Q *How can I teach my two-and-a-half-year-old son to use the Naughty Step? When he has done something really naughty like pinch me or hit me, I place him on the step and he just laughs and runs away. By that time I've lost my temper, am shouting and give up.*

A I don't think it's a matter of using the Naughty Step. It's a matter of teaching you how to use it appropriately and making sure that your son understands that certain behaviour is not acceptable. At the age of two, a child begins to learn right and wrong behaviour, and that is stipulated by the rules and boundaries you put in place. A child also needs to be acknowledged for the positive things he does. For once these have been noticed, he will continue to want to please. All kids test boundaries, especially at this age when they want their own way. Because he laughs and runs away, you feel he is not taking you seriously; but actually what he is trying to do is diffuse the situation and be in control of the discipline you are giving him and hoping that you will end up doing what you do – and that is give up. Because you have not been consistent so far, you *will* have to put him back many times and it will be important that you do not cave in. You must remain calm and follow through on each step no matter how many times. You need to be relentless. Eventually, you will end up having to use this technique less and less.

It takes a lot of persistence and patience to correct bad habits and patterns of behaviour. Many parents tolerate misbehaviour for months or even years and then, when they try the Naughty Step technique for the first time, they wonder why their child doesn't respond the way they hoped. The fact is, the longer the behaviour on both sides has been going on, the more patient and consistent you have to be to turn it around. Take a deep breath and commit to change. Keep your cool as you understand the process. No matter how long it takes, you will eventually do it.

Locking Child in Bathroom

Q *My three-and-a-half-year-old has such terrible tantrums. He doesn't stay on the Naughty Step, he laughs at me when I put him on it so I lock him in our downstairs toilet until he calms down. His behaviour isn't getting better though — he kicks and screams and punches the door. We are at our lowest parenting point.*

A I would agree that you are at your lowest parenting point when you are locking your child in a downstairs toilet. You've got to get out of this cycle. What are you going to do when he's ten years old and you lock him in that toilet and he breaks the door down? What are you going to do then?

To begin turning this around, identify where these terrible tantrums are coming from. When does he kick off? Is it because he's not getting his own way? Is it because he doesn't feel like he's able to make any choices? Is it because you're not explaining enough about what you want from him? I don't mean explaining at long length, but setting up expectations that are clear for him to meet. The more you understand what is sparking these tantrums, the better you can head them off before they begin.

Next, think about whether you are doing enough to *encourage* good behaviour so that he starts to have healthy self-esteem and he wants to achieve the more rewarded behaviour. It's all too easy for parents to get themselves into a really negative, pessimistic cycle with their children. And then they can't see any way to clean the slate and build momentum for better behaviour. To do this, you have to *notice* the small things that they are doing well that are not prompted and praise those.

Even if you think there is nothing good he is doing, there are times in the day when he's done something right – he got out of the bath when you asked, he stayed at the dining table, he walked next to the buggy when you went to the shops. Begin to notice these things and praise him: 'Thank you for listening.' 'You did a great job of walking next to me.' That's how you shape positive behaviour. And the toddler years are the most critical time for doing that.

As for his not staying on the Naughty Step, most kids won't in the beginning. They are testing whether they have to do what you say. That's why it's crucially

THE NAUGHTY STEP TECHNIQUE

◆ Before you need it, designate a spot in your house.

◆ If he misbehaves, give a warning. This gives him a chance to self-correct.

◆ If he ignores the warning, take him to the step and explain why he's there: 'You have to sit here because we don't hit.' If you choose to, tell him how long he's going to be on the step.

◆ Walk away, set the timer for one minute per year of age. You walk away so that you remain composed and so that there can be no conversation or power play on his part.

◆ He will most likely try to get up, at least at first. If he gets up, you put him back and reset the timer. Do this again and again if necessary until he can sit there for the length of time you have set.

◆ Consistently putting him back sends a very strong message that you mean what you say and are following through. Your job is to stay calm and consistent no matter how many times you have to put him on the spot. What's most important is that you are in control of this situation. You know that if he gets up, you are going to put him back. Make sure you do so silently and be aware of your body language. I have watched parents strain their eyeballs indicating 'get back' and have watched arms point to the Naughty Step as if they were signs of danger on railway tracks.

important for you to place him back no matter how many times it takes. It shows your authority in this situation – which you *are* taking control of because he is behaving in an unacceptable way. By being consistently put back on the step by you, he learns to respect and listen to your authority.

If you are a parent who says, 'But I've got to do it so many times,' then what you are showing your child is that you don't have the authority to follow through when he acts inappropriately. And so he'll just run amok with you.

- ◆ Your child may get off the step and look to play what I call Cat and Mouse, waiting for you to run and place him back over again. Ignore that if he runs back to the spot when you approach. He's already put himself back and reset the timer.

- ◆ When the timer goes off, go back and say, 'Okay, time's up.' Explain again why he was put there because, when they are very young, they are learning to remember and your actions will reinforce this.

- ◆ The apologies. I believe an apology is very important as it teaches your child to understand that he can redeem himself and take responsibility for his actions. It also allows you both to move forward.

- ◆ Hugs and kisses; giving these after a reprimand shows that you are not holding any personal grudge, but merely teaching him the importance of respecting the behaviour required, and the concept of consequences. If you follow through with the steps precisely and are consistent with following through, you will see a change of behaviour for the better.

Not Enough Space for Naughty Step?

Q *My daughter is three and she just will not listen to me or my partner. She just keeps on saying 'No' to everything we ask her to do or to stop doing. We have tried the Naughty Step, but it doesn't work as we only have a flat and the stairs where she is put are too close to the living room and kitchen. What can we do? She seems to be good for everyone else.*

A Hum, not enough space for a Naughty Step? The technique can be given anywhere. As long as you know the steps, that is all that matters. You seem to have given me a clue to the problem in the last sentence. You say she's good for everyone but the two of you. That likely means that you have not had enough consistent follow-through for her to believe you when you give her a warning. Right now she's being defiant and testing your rules and boundaries. You must turn the situation around as it is important that she learns from her parents to respectfully listen and do what is being asked of her. The size of your flat and the closeness to the kitchen do not matter to the success of the Naughty Step. She can sit in one place and you can ignore her even if you have only one room.

If you find that your daughter never listens at all unless she is getting her own way, then you will need to re-establish the rules with her. I would suggest that you also work on eye contact and tone of voice. You can't armchair-parent, shouting from the sofa up the stairs to your child to tell her to stop doing something. You must be right in front of her, face to face. That's *number one* for me in communication. Because over the years I've realised that children listen by *watching* you as well as listening to you. And you can't communicate in the same voice you use to express approval or appreciation. Your tone has to express the seriousness of the situation (see box opposite). Right now, there is no urgency to listen to what you or your partner are saying as there are no consequences that are relevant to her. If you use the excuse of not having enough space, then your daughter is faced with two parents who are not being assertive enough.

Refusing to Hug and Kiss at the End

Q *I use your Naughty Step technique with my child and I do it correctly. When it gets down to the hugs and kisses, she won't do it and I get upset. Should I leave her on the step until she gives me a kiss?*

A I'm really pleased that you are doing the Naughty Step correctly. Because in doing *all* the steps, you are teaching her the importance of consequences so she will, with age, start to think before she acts and learn the importance of right and wrong behaviour. So, well done.

The last step, to give hugs and kisses, is to teach that there's not a grudge. It's a lesson they're learning, but at this point, nine out of ten kids are still angry. They're angry because you've taken away their authority. You've taken away their control. Refusing to hug and kiss is their way of trying to gain back control and hurt you. So, no, you don't leave her on the step till she gives a kiss. Just say, 'Okay, if you don't want to kiss Mummy, that's fine.' Then move on to whatever it is you are doing next.

Won't Come Out when Naughty Step is Over

Q *My daughter is a super-stubborn almost-four-year-old. When necessary we've been using the Naughty Step. It works great! But nine times out of ten, when time is up she refuses to come out. Then what do we do? We don't want to start a new argument now that she's done her time.*

A When a child is still brewing over accepting a boundary that's been put in place, and a consequence that has followed, you may see a reluctance to shake it off. That is because your authority over-ruled her misbehaviour, her control was taken away and she may still feel slightly angry even though she has done the right things to make amends. To help her shift gears it will be important to stay casual in your tone and let her know that when she has finished sitting there she can come in and join the rest of the fun. If she says no, very nonchalantly tell her, 'Your Naughty Step's time is done now, let's move on to snack [or whatever it is you are doing].' If she refuses, leave her alone and she'll soon emerge. Stubbornness can be attached to a strong-willed temperament; however, she will learn from you that you have held no grudge and will realise soon enough it's better to get over it and move on and have fun!

Appropriate Discipline when a Child is Young

Q *My 17-month-old son has developed a bad habit of hitting me and my husband in the face – not out of anger, he thinks it's a game. I've said 'No' repeatedly but it hasn't stopped. So I put him in a playpen for time out and he just cries or screams. I am not sure he knows why he is in there. I talk to him all the time but I don't get the impression he knows what I am saying.*

A Let me explain to you what is actually happening here. Your son is hitting you to get a reaction out of you. When you get angry that he has done that, he most probably laughs to diffuse the situation. When you say the word 'No', he sees and hears disapproval by your tone and facial expression, but he may not understand why you disapprove. What is necessary is to teach him that when you are holding him it is not okay to slap you in the face. By putting him in the playpen, you have taught him that it is no longer the playpen. That action will cancel out him feeling happy to play in there. Your son is too young for a Naughty Step and I certainly wouldn't encourage a Naughty Playpen. The naughty technique needs to be implemented around two years of age when a child has enough verbal skills to understand you. Instead, this is what I suggest: when he hits you in the face, immediately move him away so you can speak to him holding him at arm's length. In a low-toned voice, tell him, 'No hitting, that's naughty.' Put him down on the floor or the sofa. He will immediately want to be picked back up again. That's when you come down to his eye level and say, 'Mummy will pick you up, but no hitting.' He will start to associate that hitting you means he gets put down. He won't want that so he will stop.

When the Naughty Step Isn't Appropriate

Q What do you do when your child doesn't listen to you in places that you can't use the Naughty Step? For example, last night in the bath, my son wouldn't stand up when I needed him to in order to rinse him off. I had to physically stand him up (killing my back in the process) and then he still wanted to sit back down.

A Parents often don't understand what behaviour is and isn't appropriate for the Naughty Step. It should be used for major offences – hitting, running off, throwing things in anger, etc. It sounds to me as if your son was having fun in the water and didn't want to stop so he wasn't listening to you. In these situations, the best action on your part is simply to end the activity if he is not going to co-operate. Tell him firmly that if he doesn't stand up, you are going to pull the plug. Literally. Explain to him that bath time is about having fun, but it is also about hygiene and keeping clean and that Mummy is here to help you do that and when it is done you can carry on playing. If he doesn't listen to your warning, open the drain so the water disappears and take him out of the bath. What he might do is begin to cry as he starts to see the water disappear and that's when you will have an open opportunity to give him the last-chance saloon – 'Listen to Mummy or you will have to get out.' If he doesn't listen, hits or otherwise acts out, then the Naughty Step would be appropriate. Remember to remind him before his next bath what happened so you give him a chance to think about his behaviour this time around. That way he can have fun in the bath, you can get your child all nice and clean, and the experience of bath time becomes a good one.

Discipline for not Listening?

Q *My son is three and does not listen. I have tried getting down to his level and asking him to do things, like put his toys away, but he does not listen. I find myself constantly bribing him and raising my voice.*

A Does your child have poor listening skills or trouble with comprehension, or is he just ignoring you because he doesn't want to do what you say? There is a big difference. You can help your child learn auditory/listening skills by playing listening games and giving him simple tasks to do. Make them very easy at first: 'Please pick up the socks and bring them to me' while he's in the same room with you. Break bigger tasks into smaller pieces. Don't ask him to pick up his toys. That's too hard. Say instead, 'Pick up the books and put them on the shelf.' When he does that, add the next task. As he gets better, you can work up to multiple items and different rooms so that by the time he's four you can say: 'Pick up your shoes and pants, put them in your room, and then come into the kitchen.' Auditory skills require repetition and your brain to remember the sequence in which they were said so that your son can hear you, take direction and follow through.

Most toddlers show oppositional defiant behaviour, but outgrow it very quickly, so I would suggest moving forward with very consistent actions on your part so that he learns to do what you're asking. You must stop bribing or this will not change. You must stop raising your voice as he is responding to your out-of-control behaviour. Children pick up on the emotions of their parents so when you get upset, so does he. If you find yourself getting angry, leave the room and take some deep breaths to calm down. Then come back and use my tips for getting toddlers to listen on page 29.

Let him know in advance the little tasks you are going to do together and when he achieves them give him descriptive praise. Thank him for his co-operation and let him know that his willingness to listen and co-operate give him time for fun things in his day. Remember to be mindful that, when tidying up, one doesn't want to be completely OCD. So perhaps putting his toys away becomes a ritual before tea time. Let him know that he will have the chance to play quietly with a toy after bath time. Always remember to explain why you are asking something of him. It will help him learn why it is important. For example, 'Let's put all your puzzle pieces back into the box because we had fun putting it together and we want to have fun doing it again, and so putting them away means we will take care of them and we won't lose any pieces.'

Partner Won't Follow the Steps

Q *Will your efforts at discipline using the Naughty Step technique still be effective even if your spouse isn't committed to doing it the correct way with you?*

A A technique needs to be done correctly for it to work. If one's spouse is not committed to doing it correctly, the technique will be compromised. So will your boundaries with your child. The message that you will be teaching your child is that she has more leeway with one parent than the other. This ultimately will sabotage the parent who is correctly using the technique and undermine them.

With discipline, what clearly is most important is that both parents are in agreement with the techniques they choose to use and with their philosophy of why they choose to use them. In other words, consistency between you is more important than one of you doing a technique 'right'. I would encourage you to use the Talking Box technique (see box below) to have a conversation about what discipline you are *both* willing to follow through consistently for the well-being of your child. You will find that it will allow you both to talk about how you want to raise your child to know the importance of respecting your family values. Because at the end of the day, you both want to raise your child to be respectful, so that everyone respects each other.

THE TALKING BOX TECHNIQUE

- Create a box and fill it with blank cards.

- Each of you writes what you would like to discuss, one item per card.

- Find a quiet time to go through the box. Cap the time to 30–60 minutes so you don't go around in circles.

- Don't move on to the next card until the previous one is resolved.

- By focusing on the question in the box, and not each other, it's easier to let go of the fear of how the other person will react.

- The important thing is to listen to how the other person feels, validate, understand and talk about a resolution, so you can move on.

- When necessary, find another time to deal with the other issues in the box. This will continue to create healthy communication between you.

Grandma not on the Same Page

Q   I have a very strong-willed three-year-old and a two-year-old who is just starting to be defiant. They are being taken care of by their grandmother during the day while my husband and I work. How can I get her to support our efforts to deal with tantrums and behaviour problems? She sabotages our efforts because she sees her way as better. I am sure that the lack of consistency is leading to more meltdowns.

A   You are right that you need to be on the same page as much as possible regarding discipline. Looking after a grandchild does not give a grandparent licence to ignore your parenting decisions even though they may feel they have earned the right. Use the Talking Box technique on page 34 to have a frank conversation with the grandmother. Let her know what you need from her in order to support you both as parents and do so with love and in a healthy fashion. Talk to her about your philosophy and why you believe in what you do and how it will positively affect the children. Ask her if there is a reason why she chooses not to support your decisions as this could be a big part of how you resolve this issue. Is it because she is the matriarch or is it because she just doesn't agree with you – is it too much for her? I know you mention that she sees her way as better, but it could be that she doesn't have the same willingness to commit as you both do.

With grandparents increasingly becoming their children's children's child-minders, there can be many opinions on raising children. For whatever reason a grandparent is taking care of your children, whether it be financial, familiarity, etc., what is important is that all the adults involved understand how you put it right for the kids' welfare. If an agreement cannot be made, finding another childcare solution is going to have to happen. Using Grandma may be convenient but the true price may be costly and damaging to all concerned, harbouring unwanted negative feelings that need not be.

Spouse Undermining Authority

(Q) *My wife and I seem to agree on how we want to raise our son, except when it comes to how we should discipline him. She always seems to undermine me, even though I'm the one who's the stay-at-home parent. This is making it difficult for me with my son during the week. What should I do?*

(A) The most important thing for you to do here is to sit down and actually talk to your wife about the situation. She's at work all day, and wants to feel like she's raising her son to her best ability when she's not at work. But the reality is you are looking after him all day. It's a similar scenario to that which nannies go through sometimes with parents who come home and undermine the nanny's discipline, which leads to the child feeling he can get away with whatever he wants to. Tell her that you're feeling undermined. Have a pact that if you've started the Naughty Step, for instance, then you're the one who follows it through. Agree that your child can't run to Mummy to be redeemed from the punishment that's being served at that time. This will keep you closer together and stop the wedge between you that your child will try to find. You don't want to be in a situation where it's Good Cop/Bad Cop.

Disagreeing with Spouse about Smacking

(Q) *I smack my child when he is naughty and the technique does seem to work. My husband disagrees, though, and it's beginning to cause a lot of tension in our relationship. I think my son picks up on the tension. How can I control my son when everything else we try doesn't work but a smack on the hand does?*

(A) I think the question here is not how do I control my son, but how do I control *myself.* You're trying to control your child's behaviour by hitting him – which is wrong. If you did that to your husband, it would be domestic violence. That's why physical punishment doesn't work. Because discipline is not about *controlling* a child. It's about guiding him to understand the rights and wrongs of his behaviour and shaping it for the better.

Your husband sees that your short fuse is leading to a volatile relationship with your child. You're in a vicious circle. Your hitting is not teaching your child proper behaviour, so he creates more naughty behaviour so you smack him again. It's not the way to establish a relationship that's healthy and loving, one where both of you enjoy being around each other. Instead he becomes fearful of you.

You need to understand how and why you're losing *your* cool. How you're getting worked up and how anger is leading *you* to hit your child. What do you feel you don't have control over? When do you feel your child plays up? Is it at a certain time of the day? Is it at a certain point in the day – meal times? Bed time? Are you allowing your child to have some independence, to make some choices? Or are you controlling *everything* to the point that your child is suffocating in this relationship? Are there outside influences that are putting more strain on the way that you're parenting at the moment? Because outside influences have enormous impact on us and we can project that anger on our child.

After you have some answers to these questions, you need to look at ways in which you can *effectively* shape your son's behaviour and encourage and praise him so you get the behaviour you want. I suggest you read not only this chapter but Hot-Button Behaviours and Bonding as well to get more insight and ideas. Your husband is not going to agree with you smacking your son in order to control his behaviour. Because objectively, what he's saying is, 'Time out. You've lost your cool. It's not working.'

Disciplining Out and About

Q *I was in the shopping centre with my two daughters, one in the buggy and one on a buggy board. My daughter wanted to get off her buggy board and push her sister along instead of me. The shopping centre was packed and she kept crashing the pushchair into the crowds so I stopped her. She got very angry and wouldn't get back on the buggy board. She hit me, then hit her sister in the pushchair, then fell on the floor and had a tantrum. A security guard came over and asked if we were okay. My baby was crying in the buggy and my toddler was crying on the shopping centre floor. It was awful. How can I enforce discipline when we are out and about? I raised my voice and shouted at my daughter and I hate myself for it.*

A This is a prime example of a situation that need not have happened *at all*, if you'd have just listened to yourself when your daughter asked to get off her buggy board. Your *first* thought was, 'This is a packed shopping centre.' So if you had just said 'No' with an explanation of *why* – 'The answer is no today because we're in a crowded shopping centre. But when we go to the park, you can do it because there'll be more space' – you could have avoided the whole problem.

Instead, you let her down because you were fearful of her having a tantrum and what you ended up with *was* a tantrum! So my first piece of advice for you is to consider the situation you are in and make a clear judgement call: 'Yes' or 'No'. Not 'Maybe'! Not, 'I'll think about it'. 'Yes' or a 'No'. Toddlers need it simple. Then you could have handled the temper tantrum if it came. You could have got down to her level on the buggy board and given her a warning: 'This is enough. I've told you no. If you're going to continue like this, when we get home, you're going to miss out on what we're doing.' You would have been able to keep her away from the baby and wheel her off because she was still on the buggy board. But in this case you said yes and then took it back, so of course your daughter got angry and had a tantrum. It was her way of showing you that she was angry with what you did. And it led to her – because of the age that she is – hitting her sister.

To avoid this in future, I would encourage you to think in advance about where you're going and prep yourself. What's the situation going to be? What is best for the safety of my children? Don't be afraid to clearly say 'No'.

Disciplining Twins

 I have four-year-old twins who like to tag team against me. How do I put them in a time out at the same time?

 Believe it or not, it is possible to do. It does take a lot of energy and you do end up going back and forth, which can feel slightly defeating. As a result, many parents get frustrated and their children end up with no discipline at all. To avoid that problem, if it becomes too much for you and you feel yourself running out of energy, I suggest you do one at a time. Start with the instigator. In twins, there's always one who's agitating the situation more and one who's happy to laugh and go along with it. Once the instigator has had her time out, then do the other. What's important is that you do it, one at a time or both together.

3

Eating and Drinking

Not eating or drinking enough, faddy eating, refusal to eat veggies, still on the bottle or the breast, dropping or spitting out food . . . toddlers can present a host of challenges to parents when it comes to food and drink. Meal times can become the battleground where a test of wills occurs, with the toddler trying to control his nervous parent, who is afraid her precious baby will not get the nourishment he needs and end up falling prey to bad eating habits.

There tend to be battles of wills when it comes to food because toddlers are having battles over everything; from what they're wearing to what they're playing with to where they're going. Food is just another arena to test their will. But it hits parents emotionally because it is such a primal issue. Indeed, I would say the whole subject of eating and drinking is *the* most fearful parenting topic. Why? Because it's instinctual. As the bird feeds the chick and the lion hunts for the cub, we human beings are programmed to feed our young. At some primal level we realise that, without proper food and hydration, the body withers away. So, deep down, parents are scared that if their children don't get proper nutrition, it will lead to hospital and fatal conditions.

At a more conscious level, establishing a healthy diet and eating patterns is important because we are creating habits that our children can carry for life. If we help them set healthy patterns from a young age, these get hardwired, and children will most likely continue to eat healthily throughout their lives.

In addition to looking to the future, parents also want to make sure that their children are getting the right nutrition *now* to grow and develop properly. To build strong bones and muscles, skin and organs. Proper nutrition is also important for speech development in babies and toddlers. When we chew, we develop our facial muscles, which are also used in speaking. We create more saliva for our digestive system.

We adults also want our children to learn to enjoy food and eating on a social level as well. And to help them avoid the eating disorders that have increased 80 per cent over the last decades in Great Britain – whether that's bulimia, anorexia, obesity or diabetes – among both girls and boys. No wonder this is such a loaded subject! But don't fear, this section is full of advice and suggestions for avoiding food pitfalls and creating healthy habits.

IN THIS CHAPTER

- **Weaning a toddler**
- **Refusing to eat**
- **Faddy eating**
- **Not eating vegetables**
- **Dropping and spitting out food**
- **The correct balance of food and liquids**
- **Getting off the beaker**
- **Two-household food battles**
- **Vomiting at meals**
- **Using cutlery**
- **Proper eating behaviour out and about**

Breast-Feeding a Two-Year-Old

Q *I have a two-year-old son who is still breast-feeding and I really want to stop. I live with my mum and have not been able to stop because she doesn't want the noise. I'm going to be moving into my own home with him in the next month and would like to know how I can stop.*

A The first step is to know that you actually want to stop and emotionally you have made this decision so this is a good step forward. Might I add it really isn't necessary any longer as he is able to receive all the nourishment he needs through the foods and fluids you will give him? There is much controversy over whether it is socially acceptable to breast-feed your child beyond a certain age. Even though this remains a parental choice, you have to think twice when you see a four-year-old toddler walking over to his mother's breast to use it for 20 seconds as a pacifier. Given the issues with your mum you might want to wait until you move out, but, if you decide to do it beforehand, it will mean that your son can deal with one transition at a time. Some mothers find themselves in similar circumstances when pregnant with another child and the first one is still hanging onto the breast.

Anyhow, let's get on to moving with weaning. I would assume he is using a beaker during the day, which would leave breast-feeding first thing in the morning and last thing at night, which is when he would seek that comfort and pacification from you in order to fall asleep. If this is not the case:

♦ **Remove the daytime feeds and do it just at night and in the morning.**

♦ **If he is not drinking cow's milk, move him to six-months-plus progress milk for several weeks so that his stomach can adjust. After a few weeks, wean him onto cow's milk. Make sure his foods are high in calcium for good teeth and bone density.**

♦ **Next remove the morning feed.**

♦ **Lastly, remove the night-time one.**

Once you stop nursing altogether, you may go through a painful period where your breasts are engorged. Do not pump to relieve the pressure as this will keep your milk supply going. Continue wearing your nursing bras until your milk production has stopped. Remember, fluid is important for both of you so stay hydrated. Congratulations! You are on to the next stage.

Refusing to Eat

Q *My two-and-a-half-year-old refuses to eat. No matter what I feed him, he throws it on the floor and shouts, 'No'. I am really worried. Can you help?*

A First, stay as composed as possible. Food refusal is a hot-button issue for mothers. We women are wired to nurture and it can feel like life or death if your little one isn't eating. But refusing food is common with toddlers and generally short-lived if you respond firmly and calmly. The more upset you get, the more it can turn into a battle of wills.

If he has suddenly decided not to eat and has been showing signs of poorliness: first, take him to the doctor and make sure there's not a medical reason for what's going on. If the doctor can't find anything and your son is within the normal weight range for his height and not lethargic, I'd guess that he's using not eating as a means of control, either to eat what he wants to eat or to use food as a means of being defiant among all the other things he is being defiant about 'right now'.

If this is what is happening, see my Plan of Action. And remember, if you try my POA and he refuses a meal, don't give him a snack 20 minutes later! That's not how to teach a child to eat a healthy breakfast, lunch and dinner with two little snacks in between. Instead he grazes throughout the day so he feels it's fine to refuse food at meal times. Stick to the three meal and two snack times to encourage proper eating.

FOOD REFUSAL PLAN OF ACTION

- ◆ Make sure you have consistent meal-time routines – set times to eat that are conducive to his body clock, which means five times per day: breakfast, lunch, dinner and two snacks.

- ◆ Sit down with him so he learns this is what you do to eat.

- ◆ Don't offer options or bargain.

- ◆ Start off with a tiny portion of carb, veg and meat (or tofu, beans, etc. if you are vegetarian), no more than what would fit on half a side plate.

- ◆ If he throws food or shouts, explain that such behaviour is not allowed. Use the Naughty Step (pages 26–27) if necessary.

- ◆ Once his time on the Naughty Step is up, reset the table rules, explaining the behaviour you want to see.

- ◆ Once his behaviour is better, you can then encourage him by compromising. Tell him that you are willing to get him down after he has eaten three spoonfuls. Please do not give in at one or two.

- ◆ Replace the negative attention he's been getting with positive by praising him to the skies for eating.

- ◆ Make sure you offer a variety of foods over the week.

- ◆ Evaluate his snacking situation. Often when parents say their kids won't eat, they mean they won't eat at meal times, but graze all day. There should be two snacks – one in between breakfast and lunch and one between lunch and tea. See the box on pages 46–47 for proper portions.

- ◆ Make sure the snacks are healthy: string cheese, wholegrain crackers, yogurt, raisin boxes, cut-up grapes, fruit in tubes. Again, make the quantity *very* small, a couple of tablespoons, especially while you are establishing meal-time eating.

- ◆ What liquids are you serving? Juices and milk can be very filling for young children. Offer diluted juices and water in between meals.

PROPER PORTIONS FOR TODDLERS

Nutritionists suggest toddlers have the following daily servings:

Ages two and three

- 60 grams protein

- 550 ml or 450 grams dairy

- 225 grams vegetables and 225 grams fruit

- 85 grams carbohydrates

- 3 tsp oils

Ages four and five

- 115 grams protein

- 825 ml or 335 grams dairy

- 340 grams vegetables and 225–340 grams fruit

- 140 grams carbohydrates

- 4 tsp oils

Protein

Chicken, eggs, fish (sole, salmon, cod and parsley, fish cakes, fish fingers/goujons, tinned fish: tuna, sardines), lamb, mince, braising steak, pork chops, meat slices (chicken, turkey, ham); tofu

Fruit and Vegetables

Fruit – satsumas, apples, grapes, raspberries, blackberries, strawberries, melon, cherries, kiwi, bananas, pineapple, oranges, peaches, nectarines, prunes, dates, figs. Vegetables – swedes, carrots, broccoli, peas, spinach, tomato, avocado, celery, courgettes, cucumber, peppers, onion, leeks, cauliflower, soft small brussels sprouts, diced mushrooms, asparagus, squash, green beans.

Carbohydrates

Wheat – pasta, rice, noodles, couscous, wheat crackers, brown bread, pitta bread, tortillas. Pulses and beans: kidney, chickpea, black-eyed, pinto, baked beans, lentils. Enriched grains, oats (porridge and cereals), potatoes, sweet potatoes.

Dairy

Milk (full-fat), cheeses, soy, yogurt.

Oils

Nuts, olive, corn, peanut, canola and other nut oils.

At least half the plate needs to be the fruits and vegetables with the grains and protein being the other half. The vegetable portion should be slightly bigger than the fruit portion as most toddlers will eat fruit for snacks during the day. The dairy is always to the side of the plate, which would be a cup of milk or a yogurt. It is important that this is accompanied by 60 minutes of run-around/exercise.

If you serve things like pizza, hot dogs, etc. they *must* be served with fruit or veg; and if you serve them for lunch or dinner then the other meal has to be one with all the balanced food groups. See page 54 for menu suggestions.

At every meal, make sure you have something from each group so the totals each day add up to the recommended amounts. We live in a world now that tells us not to eat a lot of carbs, but that doesn't apply to children. They need the energy carbs provide because their metabolism is high.

Hates Vegetables

Q *My three-and-a-half-year-old, who used to eat anything, has suddenly declared she hates every vegetable I serve. I tell her how important it is to eat vegetables but it doesn't make a difference. I don't want her to turn into a picky eater. What should I do?*

A Toddlers are very fickle in their likes and dislikes. What they like one day they decide they hate the next. There may indeed be certain vegetables she truly dislikes – even adults have preferences. However, remember a child needs to properly try a food at least 15 times to truly state she doesn't like it. And natural dislikes don't include all vegetables!

To make sure this doesn't turn into a battle, stop talking about how important it is to eat vegetables. Pleading, getting cross or giving a lecture makes the situation worse. Be as matter-of-fact as possible. Simply give one choice at every meal, 'Do you want broccoli or carrots?' If she then refuses to eat what she chose, tell her she chose it and must eat half. If she refuses to choose, tell her you will have to choose for her then. Either way a choice will be made.

If giving choices doesn't work, you might want to choose for her and mix her food together for a while to reintroduce vegetables. (See box opposite.) They don't seem as intimidating that way – tiny bits of carrot rather than several carrot sticks – and mixing the tastes may make them more palatable. Make different combinations throughout the week (see suggested plan on page 54).

Fads go the other way too. Suddenly she may find something she really, really likes and wants that all the time. That won't work either. It's your job to keep the variety there – in those three stages. Hang in there – you'll probably see preferences come and go over the next few years. Treat the situation lightly and it will pass.

THREE-STAGE FOOD PLAN OF ACTION

Stage 1– *Puree:* typically done when we are first introducing foods to babies. Veg, meat and carbs are pureed together; for instance, mashed potato, chicken and peas.

Stage 2 – *Bowl:* where you serve the same three things, but cut into tiny bits and mixed together, which they eat with a spoon. The consistency here is lumpy.

Stage 3 – *Finger food:* where you serve the same three food items in bigger sizes separately on a plate.

If your toddler is refusing to eat things separately, go back to Stage 2 or even 1 for a while.

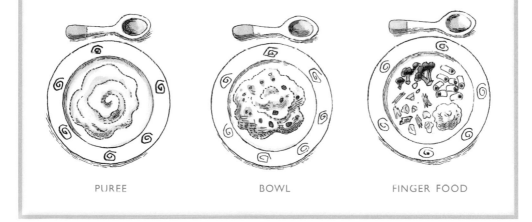

PUREE   BOWL   FINGER FOOD

Granddaughter is a Faddy Eater

Q *My two-and-a-half-year-old granddaughter won't eat anything except pasta and chicken. When she was smaller she would eat anything, now I can't even get her to try something new. I'm sure that part of the problem is her mother's eating habits. My son is divorced from my granddaughter's mum. When she's with her mother, it's all fast food because that's all she ate when she and my son were together.*

A I applaud you for wanting your grandchild to eat healthily. Of course it would be best if you, your son and your ex-daughter-in-law could all get on the same page with regards to food choices. If you find a conversation cannot happen, you can still expose your granddaughter to a wide variety of healthy choices. I would suggest my Little Chef technique. Get her involved with you in meal selection and preparation and she's more likely to want to try new things. Have her shop with you and talk about the colours, textures and tastes: 'Look at this carrot. What colour is it? Did you know carrots are crunchy? Do you know what this is? It's a pepper. What does it smell like?' Avoid giving lectures on why we should eat these things. Just get her interested in what she can see, smell and feel. Back at home, involve her in helping you cook, including perhaps washing veggies, pouring, stirring. Again, no lectures. She is too young and won't really understand. Praise and thank her for her help.

When the time comes to eat, put on her plate what has been cooked and casually say: 'Come and taste what we cooked.' If she refuses and asks for chicken and pasta, calmly explain that this is what's for dinner and keep it simple. If she still refuses, say she may leave the table but there will be no other food. If she gets hungry, she's welcome to eat what she made. I would suggest, as she likes chicken and pasta, making fresh options of the fast foods she is used to eating. For example, fish goujons and pasta with soft carrot sticks or thin slices of chicken breast with grated courgettes and sweet potato fries. It is all a step in the right direction. Be persistent moving forward and hopefully all the adults will be on the same page.

Dropping Food

Q *How can I stop my 15-month-old from dropping food over the side of the high chair deliberately? I've tried everything — ignoring it, explaining why it's not acceptable, getting her to help clear it up, ending the meal immediately, making her sit in the high chair with no food while I clear it up, and offering distraction with her favourite DVD — and she still does it, even when I'm not looking.*

TROUBLESHOOTING DROPPING FOOD

- First identify why she's dropping food. Has she eaten enough and is now bored? Or has she not eaten enough? Often when toddlers start on finger food, they can have trouble getting enough in quickly and get bored trying (see box on page 45).

- If she's eaten sufficiently and is now dropping the food, that's playing a game. Take the food away.

- If you have her on finger food and she's not eating well on the whole, then you need to go back to the Bowl stage (see box on page 49) for a while where she uses a spoon to get the food in. This will allow her to get enough nutrition.

- If she plays with her food and you take it away, make sure you don't let her fill up on snacks afterwards. Because if you do, then she learns that it's fine to play with food. Stick to the three meals and two snacks routine.

A It seems like your child has discovered that good old game 'I drop, you pick up!' Since you've already tried a number of solutions, it seems clear to me that she does it to get a reaction from you. Your actions have to be consistent. If you change them on a daily basis, it becomes a game to your child: how is Mum going to deal with this now? Repetition, on the other hand, clearly shows your child the action that will be taken if she continues.

Maybe it's time to get her out of the high chair and put her at the dining table so she can interact with you at meal times and you can focus the attention on something other than the behaviour that's causing you and your child stress!

Start afresh – buy her some exciting cutlery, a bowl, a plate and a cup. If she drops food, deal with it consistently every time with a firm 'No'. Give her lots of praise throughout meal times for eating well. This way she will get to see a different you too. Remember to make sure that she is eating at the correct times so that she is hungry and ready for it.

I don't approve of kids sitting in front of the TV while eating. However, every now and then you allow it. But the only time that should ever happen is when your kids are eating properly. It should never be used when a child is misbehaving at the table or not eating well.

Spitting Out Food

Q *How do you deal with spitting out food? My two-year-old is driving me crazy with this behaviour.*

A Take a deep breath, Mum, and dial up your patience. If he is not doing it defiantly, then it's because he doesn't want the food left hanging around in his mouth. It's a very common behaviour for this age. As soon as toddlers start to get teeth it is important that they begin to be challenged with food that gets bigger in size so that they learn to chew properly and swallow pieces of meat and veggies so that their digestion system can break it down. It also helps them to develop their facial muscles, which in turn helps with their speech development. So when you see him put a piece of food in his mouth, suck out all the juice and spit it out, he's not behaving badly. He has just chosen to chew less and continue to suck. He's just learning how to eat. It's particularly common with red meat because of the texture. It's also a slightly tougher meat than poultry.

I would suggest breaking him in slowly by going back to the bowl (or lumpy) stage (see box on page 49) with chewing by serving chicken and fish, which is softer than red meat, and cutting it up into *really* small pieces and mixing it into potatoes or rice. Over time he'll get the hang of it and you'll see the spitting disappear. Also encourage him by sitting at the table and allowing him to mimic your behaviour. He sees you chew and then he chews. As the facial muscles get stronger he will become more disciplined in chewing. His body will automatically create more saliva to help him do so. To disguise the monotony, you can have fun with it and become very animated chewing yourself. Hopefully this way you will get smiles and an empty plate.

Too Much Milk?

I am concerned that my 16-month-old son is drinking too much milk. He is not interested in eating food, he will eat some crackers or small finger food but he much prefers milk and will drink it all day if I let him. Any ideas about how to get him to start eating more food? I would really like him to eat with us at our family meals but so far he has not.

Drinking milk is a good thing as it provides calcium amongst other health nutrients, which is important for children's development and growth. However, there can be too much of a good thing. I've been told by paediatricians that too much milk can cause a delay of teeth coming in which does not give the child a chance to chew and digest solid food properly. And some children guzzle lots of milk due to the fact that it's in a bottle. Then it becomes less about milk and more about the comfort of the teat, which serves as a pacifier.

At 16 months old, you should be giving him less than what he is drinking now, as it is not allowing him to get comfortable with consuming solids. If he's still on the bottle, wean him immediately to a beaker. With a well-balanced food plan, there is no reason why your child shouldn't be content with one pint of milk per day. If he still shows no interest in food, cut his milk intake down and make sure his meal times come before the milk so that he will end up with three cups – one in the morning, one at lunch and one at night. Introduce your child to healthy food options, taking each food category slowly. And by all means, if you have a chance to sit down and do lunch together, then why not?

Not Drinking Enough

I am worried my toddler isn't getting enough fluids. To get her to drink, I have to go to her with a cup and say, 'Okay, drink the juice or the milk.' I see other kids going back to their little cups all day long, but not my child. What can I do?

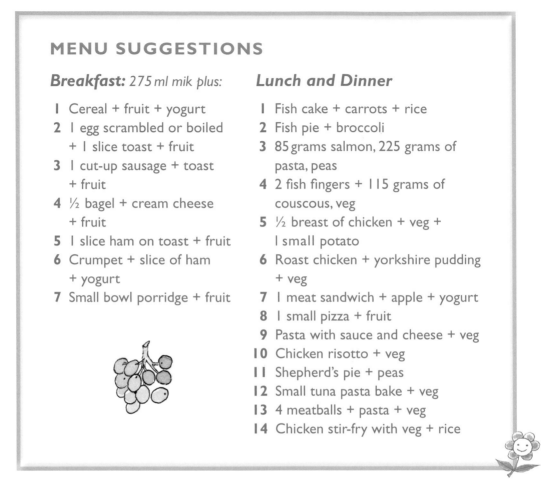

MENU SUGGESTIONS

Breakfast: *275 ml mik plus:*

1 Cereal + fruit + yogurt
2 1 egg scrambled or boiled
   + 1 slice toast + fruit
3 1 cut-up sausage + toast
   + fruit
4 ½ bagel + cream cheese
   + fruit
5 1 slice ham on toast + fruit
6 Crumpet + slice of ham
   + yogurt
7 Small bowl porridge + fruit

Lunch and Dinner

1 Fish cake + carrots + rice
2 Fish pie + broccoli
3 85 grams salmon, 225 grams of
   pasta, peas
4 2 fish fingers + 115 grams of
   couscous, veg
5 ½ breast of chicken + veg +
   1 small potato
6 Roast chicken + yorkshire pudding
   + veg
7 1 meat sandwich + apple + yogurt
8 1 small pizza + fruit
9 Pasta with sauce and cheese + veg
10 Chicken risotto + veg
11 Shepherd's pie + peas
12 Small tuna pasta bake + veg
13 4 meatballs + pasta + veg
14 Chicken stir-fry with veg + rice

Believe it or not, your question is a very common one. It's important that every child is hydrated, but at the age that your daughter is, it's random that some children need prompting and some children don't. It's really nothing to be concerned about. Some children take regular beaker drinks, but in small amounts. Others will take less drinks, but in larger amounts.

Start at meal times. Encourage her to finish her juice or milk and tell her that she can get down from the table once she finishes it. And encourage her to drink water during snack time. That's five cups right there! Nine out of ten children will be hasty to leave their juice or milk because they want to get on with playing and think they're going to miss out. Be very nonchalant in your approach and she will eventually get into the habit; making sure you leave her juice where she can easily reach it will make it easier for her. Remember, monkey see, monkey do.

Beaker Bye Bye

Q *How do I get my two-and-a-half-year-old off a beaker?*

A Congratulations on understanding that it is important to get a toddler off a beaker at about two and a half to three! By this age, he has the motor skills to handle an open cup, and beakers, over time, are bad for his teeth. With a beaker with a soft spout, the fluid is sucked directly to the top of the front teeth. If he's drinking anything with sugar in it (which includes milk and juice), this can promote tooth decay. The process is really quite simple:

◆ **Buy the 225 ml cups that have one or two handles. Have your child choose his own to make him part of the process. Tell him, 'You are a big boy now and it's time for a real cup. You get to pick your own.'**

◆ **Have him decorate it with stickers when you get home, which will help identify his cup and reduce sibling conflict.**

◆ **Throw out all the beakers in the house so you're not tempted to bring them back.**

◆ **Don't fill the cup all the way as it will make it harder to handle.**

◆ **Have him use his new cup at the table or when he's standing still.**

◆ **Encourage the 'big boy' behaviour with positive verbal praise.**

◆ **It is inevitable that there will be spillage and it's important to be casual about it. A simple 'whoops', and then a clean-up. He's learning to become more dexterous, but hasn't quite got a 'handle' on it yet.**

Two-Household Food Battles

Q *My partner and I have just started having his two-year-old son from a previous relationship live with us part-time. We are having trouble getting him to eat anything other than jam sandwiches. We've tried saying you can have pudding if you eat your dinner but it doesn't work. We have tried letting him choose what to eat but that doesn't work. We're also concerned that he has a bottle at night. His mother told us to give it to him to get him to sleep, and then leave him with it. We don't like the fact he is sucking on air through the night. What can we do?*

A It's best that all the adults talk together to agree regarding the eating rules for the little one. As you're not the two-year-old's primary carer, you should get a list of the foods he likes from his mum – this could be very telling. Have meal times together when he's with you, for example lunch times. If you offer him a choice from the list of food he likes and he doesn't make one, let him know you will make one for him. Sometimes kids don't make decisions as a technique to stall the situation. So tell him to make a decision by the time you slowly count to three. If not you will happily do it.

Unfortunately a bottle at night is very common amongst many parents, as they use the bottle as a pacifier. Children respond to the sucking reflex as they did when babies and it soothes them to sleep. But it should be taken away after the child has drunk it. This is a situation that definitely needs to be taken care of, but after the food issue is settled. His mum obviously uses the bottle as a pacifier, but it's not good for him to be sucking on a bottle of air all night. I'm led to believe that this boy is being given too many bottles and not enough food. If he's this picky at home, then his mother is probably substituting bottles of milk for food.

The best way to take away the bottle in the bed would be to give it to him as he comes out of his bath. Then take it away before he goes to bed and take him into his room and read him stories before he goes to sleep. If he cries for his bottle, just put your hands up and say 'Bottle all gone now. It's finished.' Realistically, if you want to take the bottle away completely, which is a good idea, you should talk to his mother and get her to do it as well. It would be better for him if you were all consistent. However, do know that this will lead to you having to implement a sleeping technique. See the Sleep chapter for ideas.

Vomiting at Meals

Q *My son is just over two years old and has always been a good eater. He began vomiting every day at lunch at about one and a half years old. Tests were done and luckily there were no obstructions. We were advised to leave it alone and it would likely pass. Recently, it's started again, but this time he seems to be forcing himself to gag whenever he does not want something. He does this with food that he likes as well as food that is not his favourite. I am careful with his portion sizes and make sure that I am not over-feeding him. I have tried to explain why this is unhealthy, but let's face it . . . he's two! He will tell me that I have to clean it up so I have tried to delay cleaning him up immediately to see if it will have any impact. No luck there. I am at my wits' end.*

A Having your son medically checked has eliminated that off the list. I have dealt with this situation so many times, including with twin boys. It is a form of manipulation where you become fearful as a parent and for him it is the ultimate thing to do as a last resort so you will take the food away.

Let's face it, you're right, he's only two so he's not going to understand when you explain why what he's doing is wrong. What I would do is change things around. Sit him at the table; don't pay any attention to the gagging or vomiting. Make sure he has very small meals on his plate. Talk to him while he is chewing to distract him and if he shows signs of vomiting, your face must not look alarmed and your voice needs to be confident in encouraging him to chew more so he can swallow the food.

If you start to see the gag reflex happen, I'll say it again, don't look over-alarmed, because as soon as you start to watch in horror, he will have an audience. If he vomits, calmly clean it up, and persevere with him finishing off his food before getting down. He's most likely using the vomiting as an excuse to leave the table. It is so important that you remain calm and persevere. Equally important is to give him big hugs and praise when he finishes chewing one piece of food. Eventually he will get more focused on the praise he's getting and forget about gagging for a reaction.

Using Cutlery

Q *My son's just turned 16 months old and shows absolutely no interest in using cutlery. Over the last six months, I've tried showing him how to use it as well as just left him to work it out for himself. I wonder if there's something I'm not doing right. He's my first child so I feel like I'm making things up as I go along.*

A At 16 months, he should be very comfortable using a spoon to dig into his food. You can help the process by putting your hand over his to show him how to do it. This is what I call shadowing. In addition, make sure you serve food with the consistency that would require cutlery rather than finger foods. For example, serve a chicken and apricot risotto or a good old-fashioned baked fish pie instead of chicken fingers. When you start serving foods that require cutlery exclusively, your child will begin to learn it is a necessity. Because of manual dexterity, you won't see a consistent ability to handle a fork properly until about three to four. So if you choose to serve food with consistency and then. for example, fruit for a dessert, it will help your son learn how to use cutlery alongside developing his finger control by picking up tiny fruit pieces.

Eating Properly Out and About

Q *I meet other mummies and babies for lunch sometimes and I've noticed that my toddler is always the one that is most disruptive. He eats really nicely at home but when we are out he always wants to run away from the table, and plays with his food – it's so stressful. It's the same with a picnic in the park. What can I do to change his bad habits? I don't feel like we can eat in public!*

A This question made me go, 'Aww-awww', because your toddler is just excited. At home he's in a routine in familiar surroundings and it's easier for him to remember what to do. At a restaurant or picnic, he's distracted in a beautiful way by *everything* around him – the new sights, all the other little toddlers playing. It's no different from how toddlers behave at birthday parties. Here are my tips:

- ◆ Make sure that you are eating at his established meal time.

- ◆ Let him know that you are going out with other people and he needs to eat what's in his box or plate.

- ◆ Work out with the other parents whether you are all going to have your children eat first, then play, or have a bit of play first, then eat, knowing that they will get to play again after they've eaten. Then let the kids know.

- ◆ Sit near him when he's eating so that you can encourage him.

- ◆ Be realistic with the amount that you're giving him. Excitement gets in the way of appetites. If it's a picnic, perhaps you're going to ask him to eat half a round of sandwich, some yogurt and raw veg. Then he can go and play. If he eats less than normal, that's okay.

- ◆ If you're at a restaurant be cautious of the amount of time that you're sitting around a table and order quickly.

I used to *love* taking kids for picnics in the park, especially when our weather is glorious in Great Britain. If, at tea time, we were doing a traditional British picnic, which is sandwiches and maybe a little bit of pie and a ploughman's with some yogurt and a Tupperware box of fruit, I would make sure that at lunchtime I served the meat and veg. So that come tea time, when I was having the picnic at the park, I *knew* that they would have a couple of sandwiches, a little piece of this, a little of that, and then they would be full.

4

Development

Daily mental and physical stimulation is critical for a child's brain and body development. In a very real way, we actually shape children's brains through the interactions we have with them. Their brains wire up through the relationships and experiences they have. Through interactions with parents and other carers, toddlers develop fine and gross motor skills, language, social and emotional intelligence, and life skills. That means parents play an enormously crucial role in the child's development. At the same time, it is also true that every child develops at her own pace and no one can force a child from one developmental stage to another.

Balancing these two realities — accepting the unique development of your child and making sure you are doing everything you can to nurture her development — can cause parents concern. They worry about their child's language development because a friend's toddler is already speaking in sentences and theirs is not. They see other toddlers interacting more and become concerned about their child's social development. They often don't understand that the push for independence they are experiencing with their toddler is a developmental stage.

They ask questions like: How do I know if my child is developing at the rate she should be? What sorts of activities and behaviours are 'normal' at various stages? In this chapter, I take a look at some of the most common questions parents have about development, and also tackle the issue of screen time.

IN THIS CHAPTER

- **Interaction for proper development**
- **Not talking**
- **Second language**
- **Stuttering**
- **Please and thank you**
- **Preferring playing by oneself**
- **Pushing for independence**
- **Screen time**

More Interaction Needed

Q *My home health visitor said that she thought I needed to play more with my 24-month-old to encourage her development. But I just don't know what to do! I wasn't ever a babysitter and this is my first child.*

A It is true that interacting with your baby/toddler-aged child is one of the most essential tasks required from you as a parent to support her proper motor-skill, auditory, visual, mental and emotional development. To do that, it's important to know what games and toys are age-appropriate and relevant. Follow the age recommendations on the box. Here are some easy things that I love to do, along with some tips for getting the most out of the activities:

♦ Help her learn to identify body parts by asking, 'Where is your nose? Where's your mouth?' Help her by pointing to it yourself if she doesn't get it.

♦ Common household objects can be turned into noise-makers by a simple jingle of car keys, a jar filled with rice or beans, or running water. Have her close her eyes and see if she can identify these sounds: 'What's that?' Reciting nursery rhymes and singing is also wonderful for language development, as is repeating back the sounds your child makes.

♦ Games like puzzles and shape sorters are great for visual and brain development; large wooden blocks, play dough and finger-paints are great for creative play and encompass small motor skills.

♦ 'Hide and Seek' and making tunnels out of furniture are good for motor development, rolling and catching a ball for eye and hand co-ordination.

◆ For speech development, read interactive books that require your child to do some action and have her point out and talk about what is happening. Repeat her favourite stories over and over – repetition helps learning and reading to your child will develop her knowledge of new words over three years to 50 million!

◆ Don't just put a puzzle, game or activity in front of her. She needs you to help her learn how to do it and how to engage with it, so make sure you are there, playing right alongside her. Your child will take all of the cues from you.

◆ If you notice she's becoming bored or finishes up with something quickly, it's likely the activity has now been mastered and you should move on to more challenging ones. Conversely, if she hasn't yet got the hang of a game or puzzle and abandons it out of frustration, give it time. It will be important for you to re-engage her back into the activity. Put your salesman hat back on and get her interested again.

◆ Every child develops at her own pace. Be there for that gentle encouragement because the more attention she spends on her games and toys, the more she will become engaged, the more she is engaged the more she will learn and enjoy and will want to do it all *again*. By the way, this will increase her attention span and concentration. This is necessary for her to continue learning.

◆ Between three and four, she will play more interactively with other children, learning how to share more and enjoying fun games.

◆ By age five she will know more about nature, as you teach her in detail things like bugs, flowers, animals and gardening. Board games from the familiar brands that we grew up with as kids, like Mattel, Hasbro and MB, are a lot of fun for children at this age. For example, Snakes and Ladders, Jenga and Hungry Hippos.

Not Talking

Q *My little girl is 18 months old and for some reason has stopped saying the odd word and gone back to just babbling. I keep repeating words but to no avail. All I'm getting is literally 'gaga' from her. Please help.*

A From the sound of things it would seem that your little girl has regressed a bit here. It will be important for you not to answer for her. The words that she already knows you must encourage her to keep using. If you ask her a question and answer it for her, when she already knows how to say the word, then she need not say it. Other toddlers around this age will be memorizing speech patterns and words but, as you very well know, toddlers have their own language and understand themselves! She will start to put syllables and sentences together, but first it will be single words.

To help her, you will have to be absolutely repetitive. When you say to her, for example, 'Where are your toes? Where's your ear?' make sure that you are having face time doing this. This is incredibly important because children learn words and how to speak from visually watching your mouth move as well as hearing you say the word. When you play with her with puzzles or books and point to an animal, don't expect her to be able to repeat the word; at this age she should repeat the sound it makes. Have her point out where the dog, duck and cow are, ask her what sound each makes, and do it with her. Eventually she will say the word dog and connect the sound with it. Make her aware of everyday items: 'Let Mummy help you with your jumper', 'Where are your shoes?' and 'Daddy is putting his shoes on.'

Make sure you are asking her questions, but not answering them for her. Give her time to answer. Don't make a big drama about it. Keep encouraging her to say what she wants. At lunch, ask her if she would like some juice or water and then wait for her to respond. But I'd be low-key about it. She doesn't have to say goodbye every time someone leaves, for instance. Speaking comes naturally to almost all children who don't have hearing problems. It's not something you should worry about until at least 24 months. If you aren't seeing progress in a few months and continue to be concerned, check with your home health visitor or GP.

Second Language

Q *I have a two-year-old granddaughter who speaks very well. Her mum and dad are thinking of teaching her Chinese as a second language. We have family members fluent in both languages. Will this confuse her at this age? Will she stop using her English and only speak Chinese?*

A Starting early on a second language is one of the best ways to create a bi-lingual child. What you most likely will see is an easy use of both. Typically, the child will speak to one family member in English and the other family member in the other language. If both parents are very consistent with this way of teaching it can be very successful. I have sometimes seen delayed speech with the English language if more than one language is used. The key here is to make sure that the primary language, in this case English, is more prominent because of nursery.

Stuttering

Q *All of a sudden, my three-year-old has begun stuttering. I am very worried that he has some kind of speech problem. No one in my husband's or my family is a stutterer so I don't know what to do about it. Should I take him in to be checked?*

A I want to reassure you that it is *very* common for toddlers to stutter. In fact, this stage of speech development is so common it is called pseudostuttering by experts because it is temporary. Indeed, as toddlers learn to talk, you might notice all kinds of speech issues – they may repeat certain sounds, stumble over or mispronounce words, hesitate, substitute words or sounds for the correct ones, and/or be unable to express certain sounds. You may also hear stuttering – brief repetitions of certain sounds, syllables or short words. It happens most often when a toddler is tired, excited or stressed. You may see it emerge after a move, the birth of a new baby or starting a nursery. But it can also happen for no reason at all. It's typically a phase that lasts a few months until a child outgrows it – as long as it is ignored by adults! Drawing attention to it will only make him self-conscious and may even lead to an ongoing problem. While you are waiting for the phase to end, here are some things you can do to minimise the issue:

- **Don't correct, interrupt or comment on his stuttering. Ask the other adults in his life not to correct or comment either.**

- **Don't ask him to repeat himself or tell him to calm down or slow down. Just wait patiently!**

- **Don't make him practise saying 'problematic' words or sounds. That will only draw attention to it.**

- **Talk slowly and clearly to him and give him as much time as he needs to speak.**

- **Talk to him a lot: discuss his day, talk out loud about the things he's doing and read him lots of books. A lot of listening and talking is how he will sort out the whole issue of speech!**

- **If, however, his stuttering isn't at least gradually improving after five or six months, I would suggest you take him to your GP for an evaluation. Also ensure his hearing is normal. Fortunately, true stuttering is much less common than pseudostuttering.**

Won't Say Please and Thank You

Q *My two-year-old won't say 'Ta'. He said it a couple of times six months ago but now he won't say it! We have tried 'Thank you', 'Ta' and 'Please', but he won't say any! How do I get him to start saying it again, as I know he can say 'Please' and 'Ta'!*

A Kids this age are still learning the beginnings of language. He is probably not defying you, even though it may seem that way to you. He is just not yet there in his development. To help him get there eventually, repetition and prompting are key. Don't give him what he wants until he says 'Please' and prompt 'Thank you' when he receives something. You won't believe how many times you have to prompt him before this behaviour becomes automatic – years at least! Patience on your part and lots of practice on his will eventually win the day. If he does say it, make sure you build on that. It will be very important for you to have manners too. If he gives you something, say 'Thank you' and when you give him something back, prompt with 'Thank you', implying that is what he should say. Kids basically learn through mimicking us.

Prefers Playing Alone

Q *My toddler doesn't seem very interested in playing with other children and is happy to sit and play on his own. Is something wrong with his development?*

A Your child's temperament may be one in which he likes to be and do things on his own. And that's fine, as long as he also interacts with other children. If, however, he doesn't want to play with any other children at all, then I do think you should work on his social skills.

You can encourage that by setting up one-on-one play dates so that he can get used to just one other person. Then after a while, when he's comfortable with that person, add in another child, and work your way to a big group. Some children are a bit more reserved. It takes a little time for them to people-watch before they become involved in a crowd of five or six other children.

Wants to Do Things Herself

Q What do you do when your three-year-old wants to do things for herself and won't let others help even though she can't really do it on her own? I feel that she is trying to control me.

A No, she's not trying to control you. It's a very natural part of toddler development to want to do things for yourself. So if she's showing you this through her behaviour and actions, that's a good sign. Shadow her with those things she wants to do, within reason, so that she can start to gain a sense of achievement. Yes, it will take longer. That's where parental patience comes in. Know the difference between the things she can do on her own and those she will discover she just possibly cannot do herself right now. Carve out time for teaching and practising life skills like dressing and undressing, brushing teeth and hair, mixing and stirring, so that she can learn, even if it's with frustration at first, and get it right. You see the thing is that, mentally, she knows what she wants to do but her fine motor skills and dexterity are not as polished yet. It can be a frustrating time as she strives for independence, but with adversity comes the achievement. Parents can get annoyed with cries of 'I want to do it, I want to do it.' But it's that very sense of determination that will get results in the end, so you won't have to put her clothes on when she's ten!

Screen Time

Q How much TV time is appropriate for toddlers? I confess that when I want a break, I plunk my little one down in front of the tube and turn on a kiddy show.

A British experts follow the American Academy of Pediatrics' recommendation of NO screen time for children under two and I would encourage you to minimise it as much as possible for toddlers over two. The reason is because it is through the experiences and interactions he has with other people that a child's brain develops properly and he learns the social and emotional skills he needs throughout life.

TV does not provide interaction, and interaction with people and the world around them is what toddlers need. There are studies showing that toddlers exposed to more TV are prone to aggressive behaviour and greater weight gain, and can grow into children with poor concentration, reduced athletic ability, sleep issues, an increased chance of being picked on, poor school performance and screen addictions. This ban doesn't just include TV, but also video games, iPads and computers.

SCREEN TIME SUGGESTIONS

- Please, please limit the time to 30 minutes a day total.

- Don't use the TV or iPad as a babysitter and absolutely do not put a TV or iPad in your toddler's room.

- Carve out the time during the day that you think would be most appropriate. Perhaps just after tea, or mid-morning. Remember you can always record the shows and play them back when it suits you.

- Make sure that what the child is watching is age-appropriate. There are wonderful 20- and 30-minute toddler shows and iPad games.

- Sit down with your child and talk about what is happening: 'Oh, look what the dog did! Spot opened the present. Ahhh, he was sad.' Then it becomes interactive, like a visual book.

- Talk to your child's carers. Encourage other adults in your child's life to limit his screen time, too.

- Set a good example. Be a good role model by limiting your own screen time and don't have the TV on during meal times. This is one of the most important times for toddlers to learn social skills.

That being said, I personally am not going to tell you never to do it, because people *do* do it. I myself have certainly sat with children watching entertaining animated programmes. So see the box opposite for my suggestions for reasonable use.

5

Health and Safety

It's a child's right to be kept safe and healthy. Anything below that standard is neglect and abuse. We must protect children in all ways and make health and safety decisions for them until they're old enough to be able to make those decisions themselves. This is a huge responsibility, particularly in the toddler years when you have a suddenly mobile person with absolutely no idea of the dangers the world holds. Everything from falling from heights to drowning in an inch of water to sunstroke. It can be overwhelming to think of all the possibilities.

As a parent, you really have two safety jobs at this stage. One is to absolutely ensure your child's safety inside and outside your home. The other is to begin to teach him what's safe and what's not so that eventually he will be able to take care of himself. In this chapter, I answer parents' most common questions about both these

IN THIS CHAPTER

- ◆ **Appropriate toddler bedding**
- ◆ **Dealing with fearlessness**
- ◆ **Household safety**
- ◆ **Swimming and water safety**
- ◆ **Vaccinations**
- ◆ **Sunscreen**
- ◆ **Asthma**
- ◆ **Allergies, including severe food allergies**

tasks: How do I keep my child safe from household dangers? What are the things I need to watch out for in hot weather? How do you deal with a fearless child? How do I get sunscreen on a squirming toddler?

As for health, conflicting information about vaccinations and the vast increase in asthma and allergies in young children are of particular concern to parents and the questions I answer address this uneasiness. It is my hope that what you learn here will help you stay on top of your child's health and safety, as well as increase your peace of mind.

Appropriate Bedding for Toddlers

Q *What age can you give your toddler a proper quilt and pillow? I know from the baby years that there are safety issues.*

A As you may know given your question, many babies who die from suffocation are found on their stomachs with their faces covered by soft bedding such as blankets and pillows. That's why safety experts recommend you keep blankets out of your child's cot until he's at least 12 months old and use a sleep sack or baby grobag instead. After this age, the risk of suffocation decreases because most one-year-olds are able to roll over and move blankets or quilts away from their faces. So from the age of three, a lightweight quilt and small pillow will be okay. If your child is very tiny I would suggest you continue to use a grobag or lightweight blankets.

Note: because of suffocation risk, pillows are not recommended for children under two. Actually, older toddlers don't need them either. Parents often think a pillow provides sleep comfort, not realising that their little one was doing fine without it. If you want to introduce a pillow, it's best to wait until your toddler moves from cot to bed. Go with a small one the size of an airline pillow. Stay away from feather pillows, which can set off allergies, and can smother a child if his head sinks into it while sleeping.

Getting into Everything

Q *I have a two-and-a-half-year-old son who gets into everything. I mean everything. Climbing up the TV cabinet, hands in the loo . . . It drives me crazy. He seems to be totally fearless — the other day I caught him jumping off a big rock in the park. What should I do?*

A I call kids like this Little Explorers. All toddlers explore, but some are more curious than others. And most toddlers are fearless unless they have very cautious personalities because they have no idea that they should be afraid. They don't know stoves are hot, TV cabinets can fall on them, or that they can get hurt if they fall from a tall height. They have to be taught to be safe.

HOUSEHOLD SAFETY

Everyone must toddler-proof their home. Because everyone's circumstances differ, it is up to you, carefully and room by room, to eliminate climbing, choking, falling and poisoning hazards. It will help if you get down on your knees and look at things from their height and go and get the step stool from the bathroom to see what they can reach up to. Remember, children are very clever; they will stack up books and cushions to climb up on.

Here are some of the most common dangers to consider:

◆ **Poisonous items in bathrooms, bedrooms, kitchen, laundry room and garage (all cleaning products, medicines, vitamins, paints, glues, insecticides, pet food and litter) MUST BE LOCKED AWAY out of reach. Just placing them up high is not safe, as toddlers can climb.**

◆ **Medicine can be especially dangerous as pills look like sweeties.**

◆ **Handbags should also be put out of reach as they can hold pills, toiletries and choking hazards such as coins, safety pins or hard sweets.**

◆ **All cupboards throughout the house should have safety catches so that little ones can't get at knives, plastic bags, office supplies etc.**

◆ **Bookcases and other big pieces of furniture can easily be tipped over when a toddler tries to climb on them. They should be bolted if need be.**

◆ **Cords on blinds can cause strangulation. Make sure they are short.**

◆ **A little finger in an electrical plug socket can cause electrocution. Make sure all sockets are covered.**

◆ **Toddlers can climb on furniture and tumble out of a window. Make sure all furniture and their cot are away from windows and install window locks.**

◆ **Do you have stairs he can tumble down? These should be gated.**

What you also need to understand is that a child doesn't know something's wrong the first time he tries it because his behaviour has never been challenged. So that first time he drops the toy in the loo or climbs onto the counter, it's exploration. That's your chance to explain. Say something simple like, 'That's not water we play with, that's where we do wee wees. Don't throw your toys in the toilet.' The next time it happens, step in with warnings and consequences like the Naughty Step. Because, the second time, he knows the toilet is not the place to play 'what floats'. Obviously this gives you the opportunity to let him play with water. Under your supervision, fill up the sink and put plastic cups in it.

With a Little Explorer, it is even more crucial than ever to make sure your house is toddler-proof. (See box on Household Safety opposite.) For all toddlers, the number one thing you must do to keep them safe is supervise them at all times both inside and outside the home. *Never* leave a toddler unattended. You must know where he is and what he's doing at all times. Remember, they can't tell the difference between what's safe and what's dangerous! They learn that by hearing their parents tell them repeatedly.

With a Little Explorer, make sure to teach him how to explore safely. Take him to the park and show him where he can safely climb. He obviously has lots of energy and allowing him to be so active will develop his motor skills and will use up all that spritely energy he has. Fill an empty cupboard in the kitchen and let him play with the stuff that is harmless. Remember, exploration is part of a child's development.

Note: children must always be supervised. See also Water Safety box on page 79.

Teaching Safety

Q *How do I get my son to understand the concept of 'safe'? My son thinks he's Spiderman and Batman and launches himself at walls and windows! We try to talk to him about it, and we've been through how he can break bones and injure himself, but he then does it again. Particularly at the end of the day.*

A It's clear that your son doesn't yet understand what safe means. Rather than trying to talk to him about the concept, I suggest you instead focus on making his environment safe, creating rules for what he can and cannot do, and then enforcing those rules if necessary. I love that he has the imagination of Spiderman and Batman, but whereas Spiderman jumps off buildings and he's okay, you need to make sure your son is jumping off fortresses that have cushioning. Put limitations on what he can do and where: 'I don't mind you doing that but keep away from the walls and windows.' Allow him, for instance, to jump from a bottom bunk onto a floor that has been spread with cushions and a duvet, but not from the top bunk. Outside, it's about placing him in a safe environment that allows for that kind of physical activity – playground equipment with cushioned mats, bouncy houses and ball pools – and make it clear where he can and cannot play.

Make your expectations clear and if he doesn't listen, deal with it as you would any situation where he violates a rule: a warning and then, if the warning is ignored, a consequence. See Naughty Step technique on pages 26–27 for specifics.

Age for Swimming Lessons

When is the right time to start proper swimming lessons? I want my two-year-old to learn to swim as soon as possible.

A Developmentally, most kids aren't ready for formal swimming lessons until around the age of four. But you can take her to parent/tot swimming classes before then to get her used to holding her breath and blowing bubbles. These classes are normally no longer than 30 minutes, which is ample time. What I would suggest you do is take your child swimming once a week and familiarise her with being in the water with you. Get her used to water trickling over her face, and start on building her trust with you in the water. You will soon see she will want to jump into the pool because she will trust implicitly that you are there to catch her.

It's never too soon to start teaching your toddler water safety rules. The most important one? 'Always be with an adult where there is water and never run when there is any water around because you can slip.' And make sure you are following my water safety tips inside and outside the house. See box opposite.

WATER SAFETY

A toddler can drown in a half-inch of water. Never leave a toddler unsupervised by any water, including a sink, bath or toilet.

- **Never fill a bath and walk away, even if she's in another room.**

- **After you fill the bath, always run cold water last for a couple of seconds to avoid scalding her back if she touches the tap.**

- **Make sure the toilet seat is down and the shower door is closed.**

- **Store all electrical appliances like curling irons, electric toothbrushes, hair dryers etc., away from the bath and sink to prevent electrocution.**

- **Never fill the bath higher than your child's waist while she's sitting and enforce a no standing rule unless she is getting out of the bath. Use a rubber suction mat to avoid slipping and falling.**

- **At a pool, lake, river, pond or beach, never rely on a lifeguard to watch your child. It is your responsibility to keep an eye on your child at all times. Remember, these are times when you need to be diligent and very cautious. Do not assume that because your toddler has water confidence, nothing could ever happen.**

- **If you have a paddling pool in your back garden, don't fill it more than up to her knees and never leave your child unattended. That means you have to be not just visibly near her, but physically near so you can grab her if she slips – even if she shows confidence in walking around. Bring out everything you will need in advance and place it under an umbrella: towel, sunscreen, toys, wipes, snacks etc. Don't leave for even a split second. When you're done, dump out the water, spray the pool to prevent mould and turn it upside down or deflate it. If you don't deflate it, put it where it can't fall over onto your child. Do not leave it with water in as it is too big a risk for accidental drowning.**

To Vaccinate or Not

Q *My little one is 13 months old and is due her MMR vaccination. Should I have the injections done together or separately? There has been so much talk about the vaccine that I don't know what to do. My daughter's health is paramount to me.*

A In recent years, there has been concern amongst parents that the MMR vaccination may cause autism. However, there is no conclusive evidence the MMR vaccination, taken separately or together, is a sole cause of autism. I feel very strongly that it is important for children to be immunised. Because some parents have been reluctant to do it, we certainly have seen an outbreak in whooping cough, measles and chicken pox over the last few years. I would advise you to talk to your doctor about what you feel most comfortable doing – giving three separate measles, mumps and rubella injections over time or having the one vaccination. At the end of the day, it's important for you to feel sound with the information that you're given from your doctor and also about how you go ahead and have this vaccination done.

Sunscreen Screamer

Q *You can't believe the fit my toddler pitches when I try to put on sunscreen. You'd think I was poking her with hot needles. What can I do to make this less traumatic for us both?*

A Sunscreen, like car seats, is not optional. Sunburns received as a child increase the risk of getting skin cancer later in life. So that means protection from the sun is truly a matter of life and death. The bottom line is that you have to put it on her, whether she likes it or not. Here are some tips for making it a bit easier:

◆ **She may be protesting because the type you are using stings. Some kids are more sensitive than others. Choose a hypoallergenic waterproof sunscreen of at least 30 SPF specifically designed for** children. Some sunscreens come in cream or spray, which can make a difference. Hypoallergenic means there is no scent that could irritate her skin. Make sure it provides broad-spectrum protection. This means it protects against both ultraviolet B (UVB) and ultraviolet A (UVA) rays.

♦ Let her put it on herself, with you doing follow-up to ensure full coverage. Make it a game – can you put it on your feet? Can you put it on your nose? It takes a bit longer this way, but you won't be battling a squirming child the whole time.

♦ Have her rub it on your legs too, so she sees that it is not just her who has to wear it.

♦ Also make her wear a hat and T-shirt in sunny climates. We all know the ozone layer is a force to be reckoned with.

OTHER SUNSCREEN TIPS

♦ Be sure to apply sunscreen 30 minutes before going outdoors. Then reapply it every two hours and after she gets wet.

♦ Make sure you're using enough – don't forget the back of the knees and hands, ears, neck and the tops of feet.

♦ Lips can burn too, so be sure to use lip balm that is at least SPF 30. Zinc oxide is the best.

♦ Remember, don't be lazy or cheap when applying sunscreen. Apply it to feet before putting sandals on, otherwise some parts will be burnt and others won't.

♦ Sunscreen is ridiculously expensive in the UK so look to buy these products when there are special offers. Buy in the winter as it will be cheaper than waiting until it is summertime.

Dealing with Asthma and Allergies

Q *My two-and-a-half-year-old has just been diagnosed with asthma and must use a nebuliser when it's bad. How do I get him to sit down and do the breathing treatments? He doesn't like to do it. I'm also a bit nervous about what it will mean for him in terms of fitting in with others, doing sports when he's older, and I'm scared about the danger. Asthma can be fatal!*

A I've had asthma since I was five. So I want to reassure you that with the right medications, education, a plan of action, and regular medical follow-up, most asthmatic children do just fine. They can play sports and live an active life. Unfortunately, your child is not unusual. The UK has one of the highest prevalences of childhood asthma in the world, with about 15 per cent of children affected.

It's important that you work with your doctor to control and treat your son's asthma, but it is also important that you don't label him sick, weak or an asthma 'sufferer'. He has asthma. This distinction is important because the words we use shape our children's emotional health. If you treat asthma as something terrible, your child may become afraid. If you treat it positively, he'll feel more confident. You'll also want to make sure that any child-minders and nursery schools he attends are familiar with his condition and know how to treat an attack.

Possible asthma triggers include cold air, allergens, viral infections such as colds, and tobacco smoke and other air pollutants. About 75 to 80 per cent of children with asthma also have significant allergies. If you haven't already, you may want to take him to a paediatric allergist for evaluation. If he has allergies, see my suggestions in the box opposite for minimising them.

As for the treatments, it sounds like your doctor prescribed a nebuliser. A nebuliser is an electric or battery-powered machine that turns liquid medicine into a mist that your toddler breathes into his lungs through a mask. These treatments usually take about ten minutes. You can make this easier on him in several ways:

♦ **First, show him how the machine works before he needs to use it next. Have him explore it with your supervision: 'Here's where the medicine goes, here's where we turn it on . . .' Turn it on so he can get used to the sound. Let him try on the mask. You try it on too.**

Talk in a matter-of-fact, curious way. Understanding a bit more of what is happening will help him feel more comfortable.

◆ When it's time for a treatment, let him know that, after he takes his medicine, he can do something he wants to do: 'Let's take your asthma medicine so you can then go and carry on playing with your toys.'

◆ Make it matter-of-fact, but non-negotiable. 'Time to do it!' rather than 'Do you want to do it now?'

◆ Involve him in setting it up and turning it on if the attack isn't so severe that it's an emergency.

◆ Sing to him, share a video, read a book, or otherwise distract him so that his eyes and ears can focus while the medicine is doing its job.

REDUCING HOME ALLERGENS

◆ During peak allergy season, keep your doors and windows closed.

◆ Cleanliness is crucial. Vacuum the house weekly and dust frequently with a wet cloth as this collects the dust – rather than moving it around as a dry one does. Don't forget dust collectors like blinds and light fixtures.

◆ Use a dehumidifier. If you recognise dampness or mould in your home, have it treated.

◆ Remember certain houseplants carry mould and/or pollen, so beware.

◆ Wash your child's bedding weekly in hot water.

◆ Soft toys are dust collectors. If he has a couple he loves, wash them weekly in hot water.

◆ If possible, buy allergen-proof coverings for the bed and bedding. It will help to minimise allergens.

◆ Be aware that personal hygiene products like deodorant and perfume can be irritants. Also, if you own pets or a dog that is part of the family, make sure they are regularly cleaned and their dander is vacuumed.

The bottom line is that he has to do his treatments. The more safe and comfortable you can make him feel, the easier it will become. Make sure that after the treatment you praise him for his co-operation.

Severe Food Allergies

Q *How do I protect my five-year-old daughter from her severe food allergies? I don't feel in control when she is not with me.*

A All parents want to keep their children safe. The parents I talk to who have young children with severe food allergies do often feel out of control, as other people do not take the situation as seriously as it actually is. There seems to be a lot of confusion and even flippancy around the topic, with people confusing food intolerance and food allergies. However, there is a very big difference between a non-IgE mediated allergy, which is the medical term for a food intolerance – this doesn't agree with me – and a severe allergy which can cause anaphylactic seizures and even death.

I am sure you are doing everything that you can do within your home to protect your child. Now be sure to think about the institutions that your child belongs to, whether that's play centres, churches, schools, as well as child-minders and parents of playmates. Make sure everybody your child comes in contact with understands what she is allergic to, the seriousness of the situation, and what they must do if something happens. If your child has been prescribed an EpiPen, make sure her carers know where it is and how to use it. You have to be very up-front: 'Do you think that you feel confident enough to administer this?' If it's a play date and you sense a hesitation on the part of the parent, then I would suggest that be a play date that you are part of. (See box opposite for my Severe Allergies Plan of Action.)

If you are going to leave your child somewhere at a party or a play date, I would ring up the parent in advance to let her know about your child's allergy and find out what's being served. If it's something that your child is allergic to, I would ask that they not serve it so they don't have to worry about your child accidentally eating it. If it's a function that's being held at a hall or restaurant, talk to the parent and the place as well. You should also consider using a MedicAlert ID bracelet with your child's allergy on it.

It's also important for you to speak to your five-year-old, to help her understand that certain foods can be very dangerous for her and leave her in hospital. But don't be mistaken that your child knows enough at this age that she won't be tempted to take, for example, a peanut butter cookie if she's allergic to peanuts. Children become more mindful of that as they grow older and more aware and educated. That is why it is so important for all the adults she comes in contact with to be aware of the situation so she can stay safe.

SEVERE ALLERGIES PLAN OF ACTION

Whenever you leave your child anywhere:

- **Leave an EpiPen and note with 999 emergency number and your mobile.**
- **Make sure the adults present know how to use an EpiPen and recognise the signs of anaphylactic shock.**
- **If your child goes into anaphylactic shock, have the carer administer the EpiPen, then dial 999, then call you.**

6

Hot-Button Behaviours

When children become toddlers, they develop a natural push for independence and experience a whole set of emotions they don't have words for and don't have the emotional maturity to regulate. Mix those things together and you get a whole set of difficult behaviours that can erupt out of nowhere: biting, hitting, swearing, tantruming, head-banging, whingeing, crying, screaming . . .

These behaviours can really set parents off. They're unpleasant to experience and may provoke strong emotions of anger, frustration, helplessness, and/or embarrassment. Parents often feel inadequate when their child does any of these, afraid that if they were a better parent, their child wouldn't be behaving this way. And so often these happen in public – your daughter hits her playmate while her mother, your best friend, is watching. Your son has a tantrum in front of all the relatives.

The good news is that when you learn to deal with these behaviours effectively, they will diminish and, over time, disappear. Through the way you respond to your child, combined with his becoming more mature, your toddler will learn how to regulate his feelings and express his wants in more socially acceptable ways. It's only when parents don't respond appropriately that you see behaviours such as hitting, biting, tantruming or screaming lasting into ages six, seven and beyond.

So if you are being challenged by any of these hot-button behaviours, I hope you really take my advice to heart so that you can minimise the amount of time your child spends in this phase.

What I also hope you get from reading this section is a sense of how to develop the positive behaviours you want to reinforce too. To show through modelling what acceptable behaviour is and to build on what your child is doing well so that he will want to do that even more.

IN THIS CHAPTER

- Biting
- Tantrums
- Hitting
- Refusing to share and take turns
- Bad language
- Reinforcing good behaviour
- Stopping bad habits
- Crying
- Nasty to dog
- Whingeing
- Head-banging
- Thumb-sucking
- Saying 'I hate you'
- Handling your child's anger
- Avoiding party problems and Christmas madness

Biting

Q *Help! My one-year-old son has just started biting when he's angry, especially when we try to take things away from him that he shouldn't have.*

A When a little one bites, it is certainly not exceptional. It is simply an act of sheer frustration and anger at being told he cannot have his own way. His brain simply hasn't developed enough not to act on his frustration and he doesn't have the language to express his feelings. However, this doesn't make his behaviour correct. In order to change this, you are going to set some boundaries in place and begin to teach your son what is acceptable and what is not.

When your son has got hold of something that could be a danger to him, don't just say the word 'NO' when you take it away. Explain very simply and directly why: 'No, owie, can hurt you.' If he's touching something that belongs to you or something you don't want him to have, explain politely, 'This is Mummy's' and give your child something else to play with. If he chooses not to play with it, then that is his choice. Lower your tone of voice to show it's a no-no and if your child persists, remove him from the object or place. There is no Naughty Step for a child this young as he can't understand. Simply remember your son is exploring; he is fascinated by certain objects and he is learning that some things are okay to play with and some things are not.

If, when you take something away, he bites you, remove him from you and put him down, saying in a low, firm voice, 'No bite'. He'll cry, and he may follow you if you move, then say to him short and simply, 'Owie, that hurt Mummy, kiss Mummy better.' Then pick him back up. Trust me, through this repetition, he will learn very quickly. And remember always to praise your child affectionately when he's listening to you or when you take something away and he doesn't bite.

Note: Some children bite innocently when they start to teethe. Knowing the difference is what is important so you can handle the same situation differently.

THE SPIT, BIT, HIT TECHNIQUE

I believe in handling spitting, biting and hitting the same way. They are all physical behaviours which arise from anger that hurt or are disrespectful to others. Here are the steps:

◆ **If your child is under two, say, 'No, owie, that hurts,' then put him down away from you for a few minutes. When he comes back over to you, pick him up and say, 'Owie, that hurt. Give Mummy [or whoever he hurt] a kiss.'**

◆ **If he's over two, use the Naughty Step technique (see pages 26–27).**

◆ **If he's playing and hits, spits or bites another child, use the Sideline technique (see page 127).**

Tantrums

Q *My boy turned three this month, and when I say no to him he completely loses control by screaming and hitting. For example, when we walked past a sweet stall the other day, he asked for sweets. I explained that after his lunch he could have a treat. He just threw himself on the floor screaming and shouting and hitting me! I was highly embarrassed and didn't know how to deal with the situation in public. It's almost on a daily basis that he reacts like this. What happened to my sweet boy?*

A All toddlers go through the tantrum stage and the ones that happen out and about can be the most uncomfortable for parents as they are so public. Here are my ideas for handling tantrums:

◆ **Clearly set up expectations, anticipating what your child might ask you for. For example in a supermarket, sweets. In a shopping centre, toys or a balloon. Make it clear in advance what he can and cannot have.**

◆ **If he starts to kick off and scream, make sure he cannot hurt himself on anything. Public places can be less safe. Then ignore his behaviour.**

◆ **Remind him when he can have what he wants. If he cannot have anything, repeat it and explain why.**

◆ **Don't engage in negotiations. Once you start that, you enter the game of persuasion.**

◆ **Don't get angry yourself when he's having a tantrum. Stay calm. Step emotionally outside the situation so you can handle the emotion of it all. Losing your temper will make the situation worse. Literally keep calm and carry on.**

◆ **Once the tantrum is over, follow through in giving if you stated he could have something.**

Tantrums diminish over time. How you respond to them makes the difference. You can reduce their frequency by not giving in to them in the moment and paying attention to what typically sets your child off. For example, not wanting to leave a party or the park or a friend's play date. In those circumstances you can use my Speaking Clock technique to head off a meltdown at the pass (see box below).

SPEAKING CLOCK TECHNIQUE

◆ **Give clear notice: 'In five minutes we have to leave so we can . . .' This helps the child to prepare for change and is more understandable to three-to-five-year-olds.**

◆ **If he starts to play up, offer choices to move forward: 'Do you want to put your coat on or shall I?' 'Say goodbye to everyone.'**

◆ **Sometimes toddlers don't do as you ask because they think it will stall the situation and by not saying goodbye you then cannot leave. It is their way of trying to control the situation. So if you find yourself in this predicament, just calm yourself and say, 'If you don't want to say goodbye, let's go!' One way or another they will know you are being serious and will either move reluctantly or say goodbye.**

'No Patience' Tantrums

Q *I have a 21-month-old girl who has absolutely no patience and kicks off the most horrendous temper tantrums at a volume you can hear a mile away. We just had to leave a party early as she hasn't got the patience to wait for things. When her ice cream wasn't given to her first, she threw a fit. She also had a complete meltdown in the shoe shop today as she wouldn't get her feet measured or try the shoes on. In the end the lady had to give up so we left without any shoes. I've tried the time out technique and you should hear the volume that she gets to then! I just feel so embarrassed and a complete failure!*

A Children are not born with patience, they have to be taught, and your child is still very, very young. Unfortunately, what you have been unknowingly teaching your child is that screaming and kicking will get her what she wants. You seem to be very sensitive to the volume of her screams – you mentioned them twice. My hunch is that you give in because you're uncomfortable with her screaming and are therefore reinforcing her having tantrums to get what she wants. Yes, it can be embarrassing that your child is screaming at the top of her lungs in public. But you have to put that aside and do the right thing regardless. Believe me, the people around you will, for the most part, be very understanding. They've been there with their own children – or one day will be. The sooner you stop letting her control you, the sooner the tantrums will stop.

Here's what you need to do. Follow to the letter my suggestions for tantrums in the previous answer. Do not, under any circumstances, give in to what she wants. In the shoe shop, for instance, once her tantrum is over, have her feet measured and try on shoes. At the party, after she's calm, give her the ice cream.

At home, before any event, help her learn how to behave by practising it through play: 'We're going to a party. Everyone is going to get ice cream. Let's stand in the queue and get ours.' 'We're going to the shoe shop to get new shoes. I will be the sales lady. First let me measure your foot.' Helping her practise the right behaviour beforehand will go a long way towards her being able to handle it the moment when it arises. When your child screams in public, knowing it will draw the attention of others around you, make eye contact with her and in a firm, low-toned voice let her know that you disapprove of her behaviour and proceed to carry on. When going to the hairdressers, getting shoes fitted, etc., having things to occupy her helps to distract from what would seemingly be boring.

Hitting in Public

Q *Please help me! My two-and-a-half-year-old has been constantly hitting me, mostly on my face, either when he is sitting on my lap, trying to get him dressed or if I am carrying him out in public and he wants to get down. I used to smack him on his hand to get him to stop, but he would hit me even more, so my husband and I put him on the Naughty Spot, but he laughed and hit me again when the time was up. It is so embarrassing when it happens when I'm out shopping. I just want to cry.*

A This is a very common situation. There comes a time in toddler development when they start to realise that their actions provoke a response from you one way or the other – and it's up to you to teach them which will get the positive response and which will not.

When you are out in public, he picks up on your embarrassment and knows it's the easiest time to play up to get whatever it is he wants, whether that's to get down and walk or to have the latest toy in the aisle. That's why toddlers so often act the worst out and about. They know you will give in!

Whether you are out or at home, you can teach your child the beginnings of how to communicate with you properly by first addressing the naughty behaviour and then by talking to them on their level quite matter-of-factly. That means creating a Naughty Spot or Mat and using it every time he hits you. Don't be misled by the laughter. Kids laugh on the Naughty Spot to diffuse the situation, hoping you will just let it go. And you smacking his hand to tell him to stop smacking you definitely sends a mixed message. This is one of the reasons I am against smacking to discipline children. The Naughty Spot will work if you do it consistently.

But you have to do more than just discipline. Start teaching your child how to ask for something properly by giving a clear example he can copy back to you: 'Do you want to get down? Say "Down please".' Also he's at the age when he wants to be more independent with his life skills. Dressing and carrying him all the time will seem restrictive for a child who's ready to do it for himself. Let him dress himself and walk. Encourage your child to do more you can praise him for. These actions, taken together, will turn the situation around.

More on Hitting

Q I have a two-and-a-half-year-old who hits. He does it when he doesn't get his way, when he wants attention, when we discipline him, and even just to do it. He will say, 'I am going to hit Sophie at school,' and when he sees her, he hits. I don't know where it came from. He doesn't see us hitting in our household or any other household he goes to. I don't understand what is going on, as otherwise he is a loving, caring child.

A It seems to me that your son has learnt very quickly how to receive your full attention. He chooses to openly tell you the naughty behaviour he is going to do because he is guaranteed a severe reaction.

Yes, it is true his behaviour needs to be dealt with, by giving him discipline. Follow my instructions for the Naughty Step on pages 26–27. You state very reassuringly that your son is a loving, caring child, and I am pleased to hear that you truly see that in him. So now I want you to act upon those facts. Teach him clear, simple rules that he can follow:

1. **Be kind with your words**

2. **Share and play nicely**

3. **No hurting anyone**

Give praise and reward when he follows the rules. He will learn that positive behaviour is far more rewarding than negative attention. I would also make sure that if he tells you he is going to hit somebody and he proceeds to follow through, tell him he will lose the privilege of doing what his siblings are going to do. That will have a greater impact on him as he will want to join in on the fun.

Sharing

Q *My three-year-old has a terrible time sharing. Toys, treats — he wants them all to himself. He screams and refuses to share no matter what I say. It's a constant litany of 'mine, mine, mine'. Help!*

A Sharing is one of those crucial social skills that must be taught. You are going to need patience because it is not something that will happen overnight. Hang in there; with repeated practice he'll eventually be able to do it. Just know that you will be prompting for a long time and will need to exhibit lots of sharing opportunities for him to learn and understand.

The best way to start teaching him to share is to make him do exactly that at every opportunity with books, crayons, toys, outdoor toys etc. See the box for my Timed Sharing technique on page 96. Given the issues your son has with sharing, be sure to practise a lot!

In addition to role-playing, be sure to prep him before a play date begins or, if it happens with siblings, when they start to do something. Explain that it will be fun to play together and share. If he starts to get very possessive of his toy, 'But it's mine! It's mine! It's mine'!, be firm and explain it's good manners to share and that sharing means your friends can come around and play. Get a timer and explain to your son that he can play with the toy till the timer goes off and then he must let his friend play with it. Tell him that when everyone has had a turn, he can have it back. He will be used to this because you have practised it with him.

When the timer goes off, encourage him to hand the toy to the other person. Don't try to take it out of his hand or you will end up in a tug of war. Remind him that the time is up and he needs to hand it over and that he will get it back. Use the timer with the other child as well, so that the time is equal for everyone. When everyone has had a turn, return the toy to your son. Also, have your child play games with a friend that take two to play. That way he instantaneously sees the fun of playing with a toy together.

I also believe it's fine for a toddler to have a special lovey or toy that he doesn't have to share, as long as it is one thing and not every toy. This should be put away before a play date. Explain: 'We're going to put that away and share your other toys,' because sometimes a particular toy can have sentimental value.

If you are taking along a load of sand-pit toys to the park, explain to your toddler before you go that he'll be sharing them with others. Involve him in the process of what to bring to share so he'll be prepared.

TIMED SHARING TECHNIQUE

◆ Have one toy and tell him you're going to share.

◆ Show him a timer and explain that when it pings, you will play with the toy.

◆ Give him the toy, set the timer for five minutes.

◆ When it pings, reset the timer for five minutes, you play.

◆ Switch again when the timer goes off.

◆ This enables him to see that the time he has to wait is not endless. He will get the toy back, which allows him to relax and share.

◆ Increase the time as he gets the idea.

Taking Turns

Q *How can I help my two-and-a-half-year-old learn to take turns? She does not wait patiently, but rather grabs what she wants or pushes her way onto the trike or slide.*

A Taking turns is a form of sharing that requires a lot of patience and mental skill for toddlers. It's important that you teach your child this social skill because there is a lot of waiting your turn in life. Make it into a game that you play with her before she must interact with other toddlers. See the box opposite for my Taking Turns technique. Create as many occasions to practise with you as possible. A simple one is to take turns colouring in a picture in a colouring book: you colour for two minutes, and then I do. Practice and prompting over time will turn this around eventually.

> **TAKING TURNS TECHNIQUE**
>
> ◆ 'Your Turn': give puzzle to your child.
>
> ◆ 'Now my turn': I do the puzzle.
>
> ◆ She'll see the switch back and forth and how she has to wait until it's her turn. Eventually she'll be able to do it with friends.

Bad Language

Q *We have a very bright and generally very well-behaved little boy. We use the Naughty Step for unacceptable behaviour and it works well. Recently he started using language like poopy head, poopy bum, etc. We did not do anything about it to start with because we thought we were just going to give it more credence. However, I am wondering whether we should start using the Naughty Step as it is not stopping and seems to be less about the shock value and more about being cheeky.*

A Most toddlers will play around with language like your young one is doing now. Normally it is done for pure fun and jest. They are starting to discover that certain words provoke a response in others. You might even notice how they will belly-laugh and put their hands over their mouths in a fun way as they say it, laughing because the word sounds funny.

If, however, you feel that your child's attitude has changed when he uses such language, that he is actually directing it personally at you, calling you poopy bum, then you have the choice of whether to use the Naughty Step or not. It all depends on what your family rules and values are. If you do, make it clear that it is a family rule: 'We don't use language like that.'

I would also look closely at what is provoking this attitude. My sense is that your child needs to continue growing more independence within the boundaries and limitations you set. How can you give him more responsibility for himself? Make sure you are keeping up with his life skills so that he has a sense of accomplishment and move him on once he masters one skill – dressing, for instance – then help him go on to the next – putting on his shoes and fastening them. An increased sense of independence will help him not feel so controlled and therefore may reduce the bad language.

Reward Too!

Q   *I am trying to get my three-year-old to obey me. He is quite defiant and spends a lot of time on the Naughty Step. What else can I be doing to turn the situation around?*

A   I don't want any parents reading this book to get the feeling that it is *only* discipline that you need to implement when toddlers are acting up. Toddlers also *need* to be encouraged to learn proper behaviour. And we do this by praise and reward. Be descriptive with your praise; let him know exactly what he did that is getting rewarded. It sends a clear message of proper behaviour and he will be eager to do it again. Visual reward charts also help. So does a Reward Jar:

- ◆ **Get a large, clear plastic jar.**

- ◆ **Buy some small coloured balls that fit in the jar but are too large to swallow.**

- ◆ **He starts with three balls in the jar. Each time he does what you ask, he gets to add another ball to the jar.**

- ◆ **Each time he listens and co-operates he gets a new ball in the jar.**

- ◆ **When he reaches ten balls, he is given a chosen reward.**

This will literally get the ball rolling (excuse the pun!) and turn the negative behaviour around.

How Do You Stop Bad Habits?

Q *For about a year, my three-year-old has had a habit of clenching her teeth if she is really excited or tired, and for about the past month she's started fiddling with her eyebrows. She is a very energetic little girl and it almost seems like she can't get all her energy out. She sleeps really well at night, about 11 to 12 hours, and goes to bed with no problems. She expresses herself extremely well and has great co-ordination. I've noticed that if she is playing with other kids or there's a lot going on, the eyebrow-fiddling gets worse. She doesn't hurt herself or pull out the hairs, just frantically fiddles. She even at times fiddles with her father's and my eyebrows. I have just been ignoring the habit and hoping she will grow out of it. Am I doing the right thing?*

A It would seem that your daughter's development is thriving on all levels. However, there is something going on for her that she's expressing through these two habits. Bruxism is the medical term for clenching or grinding teeth. Some children do this when they are stressed, hyperactive, or really tired, angry or frustrated. And there is no doubt that your child is getting some kind of soothing satisfaction from fiddling with her eyebrows. However, I wouldn't encourage her to do the same with yours or her father's, as it could accentuate this habit. Just remove her hand when she starts with you.

I'm glad you've started to take note of when she does this the most because this is the area I want you to concentrate on more. Write down when this behaviour occurs so that you can understand the pattern of the underlying problem, and then work on breaking the cycle by teaching her to cope another way. You write that she does it when there's a lot going on – do you have a sense of what's happening inside her? Does a lot of noise or activity create a feeling of panic? When she is playing with other kids and you see the eyebrow-fiddling get worse, does she feel frustrated or afraid? Understanding the why will point you to the solution. Perhaps, for instance, you need to work on her social skills so that she learns how to interact with friends one to one and then in bigger circles in a more comfortable state of mind.

One last thing to note: most toddlers do grow out of such habits as they mature emotionally and become more consciously aware of themselves and others, which is normally at around six or seven years old.

Crying Child

Q *My two-and-a-half-year-old is constantly crying. How do I get her to stop?*

A You can't force a toddler to stop crying. Nor should she ever be disciplined for crying. It's her way of expressing her feelings – at this point in her development, perhaps the only way she has. Rather than focusing on getting her to stop, I would encourage you to start to pay attention to what she's trying to tell you. Toddlers can cry when they are angry, sad or afraid. They cry when they are sick. They cry when they are tired. They cry when they get physically hurt. I don't see in your question any awareness of the messages she's trying to send. The more you understand why she's crying, the more accurately you will be able to respond to her.

Parents of toddlers often make three kinds of mistakes when their child cries. The first is to assume it's a manipulation that must be stopped with discipline rather than an emotional expression to be understood. Yes, some toddlers turn on the crocodile tears to try and get what they want. But to assume that's always why they are crying gets in the way of your providing empathy and support.

The second common mistake is to do anything, reasonable or unreasonable, to get the tears to stop – bribing, distracting with treats, giving up what you were going to do because she's unhappy. That actually teaches them to manipulate you with crying and doesn't help build up their resilience to deal with frustration.

The third mistake is to treat the toddler like an adult and give her the third degree about what the problem is: 'What's wrong? Are you sad because we're leaving? Or is it because you don't like the child-minder? Or are you sick?' It's your job to figure out what's going on and respond to the true need. Asking such a young child will only confuse her or plant ideas in her head.

Dealing effectively with crying is all about understanding your child. For instance, 'She doesn't usually cry at lunch,' assessing the situation – 'Oh, it's 30 minutes past nap time' – and then using your best judgement as to what is needed – 'I'd better wrap up my conversation with my friend and get her home to bed.' Depending on what you figure out, sometimes the best approach is to ignore crying. Sometimes you might respond with a hug. Sometimes a distraction is what's needed. Sometimes an acknowledgement of how they are feeling. You can't respond well if you don't understand what's going on.

Over the years, you should see crying diminishing as she learns better how to express herself. You can help her in that process when she gets a bit older, around three to four, by showing pictures of people in various emotional states and helping her identify their feelings, as well as talking to her about how she is feeling.

Nasty to the Dog

Q *My three-year-old son loves our dog but is extremely rough with him. He is constantly wrestling, pulling his tail, and sometimes even kicking or hitting the dog. The dog is very tolerant of his behaviour, but I can't seem to get him to stop.*

A This is animal abuse, so you must curb his bullyish behaviour and teach him the proper way to treat the dog. Your child is old enough to understand that his behaviour is unacceptable.

Parents ask me all the time how to teach their child not to rough-house with a pet. It's no different than teaching them how to treat a baby. Never leave a toddler alone with a dog. Demonstrate how to be gentle and kind, then warn and put the Naughty Step in place every time he bullies the dog. In addition to teaching him what NOT to do, I would give your son some responsibility for caring for the dog. Let him give the dog its food and water. Acquaint him with the way in which we take care of an animal. Reward him with praise for his kind behaviour towards the dog.

In addition, make sure you work on his social skills on play dates both at the house and on the playground. How does he interact with other children? Make sure he is not acting aggressively. Children who are bullyish towards pets are often that way with other kids as well. If you see similar behaviour with children, be sure to institute discipline straight away.

Whingeing

Q *Why does my two-and-a-half-year-old whinge when she wants something instead of asking me? She can speak and tell me what she wants, but chooses to whinge instead. It's driving me crazy!*

A Whingeing or whining often shows up around three, so your child is a bit ahead of the curve. It can signal that she feels out of control or overwhelmed, or is hungry or tired. But it can happen for no reason that you can figure out. The key is to nip this behaviour in the bud so that she starts talking again.

Parents often say, 'Stop whingeing' to their toddler, which is a waste of breath because she doesn't understand. Instead, mirror back the tone so that she gets what you mean. Say, 'Ask properly. Use your proper voice, not like this . . .' Then caricature back to her how she sounds in a humorous way with an exaggerated face. Then ask her to say it in her proper voice. Make sure you do not respond to what she is saying until she says it in her conversational voice. Otherwise you will be reinforcing whingeing and it will go on longer. Kids keep whingeing because parents give in to it.

Head-Banging

Q *I have a 19-month-old little boy who has a terrible habit of head-banging out of frustration. He is my fourth-born but he is the only one to do this. I ignore it and it usually lasts just seconds, but I obviously worry about any damage he may be doing to his head!*

A Head-banging is one of the many ways toddlers try to get what they want. I would not recommend ignoring it. Distract him if possible and if it happens anyway, keep your child safe by putting a pillow on the floor or against the wall he's hitting himself on. Once it's over, move on without comment. Make sure you don't give in to whatever it is that he's trying to get through his head-banging. If he doesn't get what he wants from doing it, it will stop.

Thumb-Sucking

Q *My two-and-a-half-year-old sucks his thumb and it drives me crazy. I am constantly pulling it out of his mouth but as soon as I turn around, it's back in. My mother suggested I try putting gloves on him. What do you think?*

A Sucking on thumbs, fingers or dummies is how babies self-soothe. It's an instinct that is associated with the sucking reflex. So it's not surprising when you continue to see this behaviour in the toddler years. That's why, no matter what method you may try – glove-wearing, painting a bitter substance on the thumb – you can't really stop a child from thumb-sucking unless he wants to. Some kids stop as they get older because they get peer pressure. Other kids outgrow it. They find something else to occupy them or don't need soothing in that way any more.

Unfortunately, your annoyance can set up a power struggle that can reinforce the behaviour and the stress of your attention on it can actually increase its occurrence. So I have some suggestions for you. First, remember that no teenager sucks his thumb – or at least, not in public. Meaning this behaviour will pass eventually when the child becomes more emotionally mature.

THUMB-SUCKING ADVICE

In addition to looking at the underlying reasons for his thumb-sucking and dealing with those:

* **Keep his thumb healthy because the skin can shrivel and smell from being in saliva all day. Wash and dry thoroughly and put Vaseline on it to prevent cracking and splitting.**

* **Keep the nail short to avoid injuring the mouth.**

* **To help increase his awareness of what he's doing without getting into a power struggle, say in a calm, quiet voice, 'Please take your thumb out of your mouth.' Then move on.**

In the meantime, you can reduce thumb-sucking by recognising when and why he does it. Does he thumb-suck because he's bored? Does he do it when he's tired to help himself fall asleep? Does it happen when he's going into new situations as a way to self-soothe? Does he do it purely for pleasure because it feels good on the roof of the mouth? If you understand when he thumb-sucks, you can help him with that issue in other ways. If it's boredom, you can help him find something interesting to do. If it's the stress of a new situation, you can rehearse what will happen before you do something. Help him learn other ways of dealing with stress.

'I Hate You'

Q *My four-year-old is constantly telling me 'I hate you' when he doesn't get his way. We use the Naughty Step for unacceptable behaviour, but what is the best way to stop the constant rant of 'I hate you'? We have tried to explain to him that this is not a nice or acceptable thing to say.*

A The best way to stop the constant rag of 'I hate you' is to not allow it to penetrate. Ignore it. He says it because he knows that it gets to you emotionally. Your son is just learning that there are things he gets and things he doesn't – and that's just plain old life. At this age, such comments are used to convey feelings of wanted independence and the struggle to get more. He doesn't really mean it. It's amazing how children at such a young age can so quickly learn the art of manipulating with words! Translation: 'I hate you' equals 'I want my own way and you are stopping me.'

Screaming When You Say No

Q *My daughter is three and a half. When you tell her 'No' or she doesn't get what she wants, she SCREAMS! So loud I'm afraid someone is going to call the police on me. And she will keep it going for ten minutes or more. I have tried time outs, I have tried putting her in her room, but it never stops.*

A My concern is the phrase 'I have tried', because you may have tried, but I don't know if you've followed through. My hunch is that you end up giving in because you can't stand the sound and that reinforces her screaming. I would try actively ignoring and let the screaming run its course. By ignoring, I mean absolutely, totally ignore. Leave the room. No talking to her whatsoever – no trying to figure out what's wrong, no trying to reason with her, no threats. Just a simple, 'I am not going to talk to you when you scream,' and leave. It may take a while but if she really gets no attention for screaming, it will go away.

One other thought. It's very common for a three-and-a-half-year-old to want to do things her own way. Maybe you're not allowing her enough independence. Are you letting her choose her own clothes, dress herself, play with things she wants to? And don't forget to encourage the positive things that your daughter does. Sometimes we forget that encouragement of the positive is just as important, if not more so, than simply correcting negative behaviour.

Handling Your Child's Anger

Q *When my three-year-old is told 'No' or she can't have what she wants, she gets so angry. She hits, screams, throws things. I find myself giving in to avoid her anger. I know that's not right. What should I do?*

A First, congratulations on your honesty. That's the first step towards change. Toddlers don't have the ability to regulate or verbally express or articulate their feelings – that's partly why the toddler years are so intense and challenging. If they are angry, they show it by lashing out – grabbing, hitting, biting, spitting . . . each child has her own particular favourites. That's in effect what a tantrum is, an attempt on your child's part to say, 'I'm angry'.

Because a child isn't born with the ability to self-regulate, you must teach her how to identify and handle her emotions, particularly anger. Hopefully, if you understand it as part of your job as a parent, it will become easier for you in the moment to step into the storm and help her learn how to manage her anger, even though it may not be pleasant. Avoiding this task because you don't want to have your child angry with you may result in raising a person who flies into rages as an adult, thinking that is perfectly acceptable. Anger is an emotion that she owns and will learn in time to have more discipline over. When you see her become angry, you can help her to calm down by giving her space and a moment. However, you must discipline your daughter when, as a result of her anger, she hurts or attempts to hurt someone or something. Otherwise, without consequences, she will not have any incentive to learn to manage her anger. See the Naughty Step technique on pages 26–27.

After she's calmed down, be sure to talk to her about what happened and what else she can do to deal with her anger: 'You got angry when Alex took your crayon. That's okay to feel. But it's not okay to hit. Use your words next time and say, "I don't like it that you took my crayon."' Keep it very simple and understand that you will likely have to repeat this many times before you see lasting change.

As she gets older and more familiar with her feelings of anger, you can teach her the Blow Out Anger technique (see box below). This works well for four- and five-year-olds so they can learn to breathe and calm down. And no matter what, be sure to praise her to the skies when she expresses her feelings in words rather than actions.

BLOW OUT ANGER TECHNIQUE

♦ **Get down to her level, face to face, about two feet apart, and make eye contact.**

♦ **Ask her to copy you. Then breathe loudly and slowly through your nose to the count of three and breathe out loudly through your mouth. (You should slightly exaggerate this exercise so she can see and hear clearly what you are doing.)**

♦ **Repeat five times, coaching her to do it with you, using your right hand to count the number of times you've done it.**

♦ **The focus and concentration needed to do this diffuses the anger she is feeling and starts to help her have more self-discipline.**

Avoiding Party Problems

Q *My child is about to turn two and I'd like to have a few mates from his play group over for a birthday party. What should I do to make it as happy and trouble-free as possible? I can just imagine tantrums, crying over toys, etc.*

A First of all, keep it simple. Two hours for this age is ample, either mid-morning or mid-afternoon. That's when they are most rested. And keep the group small – one handful or two. What you're trying to provide is a chance for your two-year-old to have a special time for his birthday, not create a three-ring circus. There's no need for clowns, magicians, bouncy houses or other expensive party fare. Kids of this age are often afraid of clowns and they don't need more than a place to play and some food to be happy. Save your money for those things when he's older.

Plan on half an hour for a couple of activities, for example Pass the Parcel, where one can have light music and the parents can be involved. Musical Bumps, half an hour for food and including cake and/or ice cream, then half an hour for running around. If you can go outside for the last 30 minutes, great, and if the weather allows you to do the whole event in a park or garden, even better – make it a picnic party. As you know, kids this age need plenty of space to move.

Keep the food simple too. No need to knock yourself out with too many choices. Parents of two-year-olds will naturally tend to hang around the whole time, so prepare some light adult snacks and drinks as well. Most parents are happy to step in if they see any squabbling happening at a party and tend to make things go more smoothly.

Prepare your son by explaining that a party means sharing his toys and allow him to put away one or two special things he doesn't want to share. But don't be surprised if, even with your advanced planning, there end up being meltdowns or squabbles. You haven't failed. This is totally normal for this age and stage. Toddlers are just learning to get along with others and parties are a great place to practise.

Opening all the Presents

Q *Help! My five-year-old gets so excited when she receives presents that she often wants to open them all and I lose track of who sent what. Then it is embarrassing when it comes to sending thank-yous. How do I get her to be more patient at a time that is so exciting for her, as she has a birthday coming up?*

A What kid doesn't get excited on their birthday? Their favourite friends are coming through the door holding birthday gifts to open!!! Here is what I suggest: two weeks before her birthday, have her draw a picture of what she thinks her birthday party will look like and have her put her name on it. Make these into thank-you cards that she will use for her birthday presents. Then when her birthday comes around, have a table the gifts clearly go on and let her know that there will be the opportunity to open three presents after she has blown out her birthday cake candles. This way she gets to open some and you get to track who the gifts are from. Do three at the party, three after bath time that evening, and then perhaps she can have a present-opening day the day after. That should do the trick.

Fear of People at Parties

Q *My toddler gets very upset in a room with more than five people in it. She screams and yells, then will cry and get upset. It's hard when we go to family events or friends' parties as she doesn't want to go into other people's homes and won't be put down or leave my arms. How do I build up her confidence? It's becoming a real problem.*

A Between the ages of two and three, children again go through separation anxiety, in which they can feel tentative going off on their own. To help her through this stage, it's important for her to get used to playing with others while you are still in the same room. Before you venture out to parties, I suggest you begin to have family members and friends over to your home. You may have one other mother come round with her kids and then the grandparents may come round. It needs to be regular interaction, at least once a week, so she gets familiar with having people around in her environment.

Go out with her as well. Go to the library for the reading class every week. Go to the church that has the play time every Friday from one till two. Get her used to being around people with you still there so that she's not overwhelmed by the stimulation of people and noise. The more people that are around your child, the more accepting she will become. So that when you go to a family event and/or a party, she will comfortable.

If, however, you do this familiarising and you still see a possessiveness in her, an 'I don't want to share you with anybody else' attitude, that's a boundary issue. You can tell it's about boundaries if, when you're on the phone, she's always trying to get your attention or you can never talk to anybody else when she's around. Or if she's constantly encroaching on your space and wants whatever it is you have. If that's the case, see my answer to learning boundaries on page 127.

Avoiding Christmas Madness

Q *I've got three kids, ages five, three and 18 months. How do I avoid the Christmas madness and ensure happy holidays for all? I can feel the pressure building back in September!*

A Before you start worrying that everything needs to be perfect, sit down and think about what really makes Christmas special for you. Don't try to live up to other people's expectations. Christmas is not about who spends the most, it is about spending quality time together and creating magic that cannot be bought at a toy shop. Please don't feel guilty or put unnecessary pressure on yourself. Kids need your love, time and attention. Those things last for a lifetime, unlike a toy that they will be bored with after a month. All year we are rushing around, too busy to spend any real time together – Christmas is a chance for you to get back some of that family togetherness.

So with your priorities straight, the next thing you need to do is agree with your partner on a budget. Work out what you can afford and then set yourself limits. Spending more than you can afford will only stress you out. It is not difficult to create magic at Christmas on a budget, especially with young children. Supermarkets have some great toys for little ones at very reasonable prices. Prioritise your spending from day one and make sacrifices. If you smoke, cut down or, even better, give up. Put the money you would have spent on your vices in a jar and see it all add up. Start buying pressies in September so you are not cramming all the shopping in at the last minute and get stuck with a big bill in January.

Adverts for the latest toy will provoke a shout of 'I want that' from any child over two, but the chances are they won't remember what it was in five minutes. Rather than having the kids make a list for Santa, make a list of presents you can afford and turn it into a list from Santa. It's up to you to create a bit of magic, so take time to decorate the list to make it look authentic. Stain the paper using teabags to make it look old, tie it up with a ribbon or set up a treasure hunt to find it. Make a big fuss of the fact that the letter has come from Santa and allow the two older ones to choose a gift from the list. When it appears under the tree, they will be thrilled.

Kids are bound to be excited and restless in the run-up to Christmas, but there are plenty of activities you can involve them in to keep them occupied:

FUN PRE-CHRISTMAS ACTIVITIES WITH TODDLERS

- **Spend an afternoon making Christmas decorations. Make some popcorn and get them to make popcorn strings or cut up some paper and make paper chains. Or buy a bag of cranberries and make cranberry chains.**

- **Take the kids down to the local park and spend some time collecting pine cones. Even an 18-month-old can pick things up! When you get them home the older ones can use paint, glue and glitter to decorate them to make table decorations for Christmas Day.**

- **Decorate the mantelpiece with cotton wool snow.**

- **Bake and decorate Christmas cookies together.**

- **Help your toddler make Christmas cards with finger-paints or chunky crayons. I used to love to have Nanny time making cards, and Grandma and the other relatives will be thrilled to receive them.**

To make the actual day easier on yourself, prepare as much food as you can beforehand. Traditional English dishes, like lemon meringues and trifles and crumbles, can be made in advance and stored in the fridge. Stuffing can be made in advance, turkeys can be soaked and prepped, brussels sprouts, potatoes and other veg can be peeled and put in saucepans of cold water until it's time to cook them.

As for getting the kids to bed on Christmas Eve, this is the one night of the year when you really have to roll with it. Try to remain calm and patient. Stick with their usual bed-time routine, but maybe start half an hour earlier to allow for things like the Christmas ritual of leaving out mince pies and carrots for Santa and Rudolph. Reading Christmas books as the bed-time story is a good idea, because they usually end with the child in the story going to sleep so that

Santa will come. Accept that they may take longer to settle and relax about it. As long as they are in their rooms, you can get on with whatever last-minute preparations you need to make. Once they are in bed, exchange presents with your partner and take some time together so that Christmas morning can be all about the kids.

On the day itself, try to follow your kids' normal routine within reason – if they usually need a nap in the afternoon, they will need one on Christmas Day. Let them take one of their toys upstairs with them and put it by the bed so they know they can play with it when they wake up. If the older kids act up, make sure you give a warning and then institute discipline if necessary. Allowing them to spin out of control because you don't want to ruin Christmas can lead to unhappier holidays than necessary for all concerned. If someone needs disciplining, do it and then go back to enjoying the day. The same with tantrums.

HAPPY CHRISTMAS HOLIDAYS WITH BLENDED AND DIVORCED FAMILIES

Many families stress out about Christmas when they have two-parent households. The main thing here is to consider both families. It is really important that everyone is willing to co-operate. If you can't be amicable for the rest of the year, pull your socks up and have some good will at Christmas. If you arrange a time to drop kids off or pick them up, stick to it. Come to an agreement about where the kids will be on which day and make the most of your time with them.

One of the classic complaints is that the other parent has bought the present they wanted to give. That kind of squabbling has nothing to do with the child and everything to do with your own insecurities or issues – if anything, you should club together and get your kids what they really want. If you are bringing two sets of kids together for the first Christmas think about choosing neutral turf. By spending the day, or even just lunch on neutral ground you will prevent any one set of kids from feeling at a disadvantage. Try buying a game that they can all play together that will encourage them to mix.

If they occur, follow my advice on pages 90–91 and move on. Everyone will understand – if they've brought their kids, most likely they will be dealing with similar issues sometime during the day. And keep the togetherness time short if there are lots of young kids involved – a couple of hours at most.

If you are having people over for a meal, don't be afraid to ask relatives or friends to muck in. If Mum is getting lunch ready, then Dad can take the kids to the park for an hour to get some fresh air and work up an appetite, or vice versa. When it comes to meals, be realistic about what you want your kids to eat. Avoid letting them fill up on chocolates and treats in the morning and don't pile their plates too high – be conscious of appropriate portions.

Don't feel you have to fill Boxing Day with all kinds of activities. Kids this age will still be excited about their new toys. Just because 25 December is over and done with, it doesn't mean you have to draw a line under Christmas straight away. Instead of taking all the lights down, move them into the kids' rooms for a week or so. When the time comes to take down the Christmas cards, use them to make puzzles. Cut the pictures in half, shuffle them and get your kids to match them up again.

Bottom line: remember, you don't have to cover the floor in expensive gifts to have a good time at Christmas. Give your children your time – that's what they'll remember as adults.

7

Life Skills

Part of your job during the toddler years is to teach your child life skills. These skills run the gamut from practical things like learning to dress and brush their own teeth and hair, putting away toys and beginning to do chores, to social skills like playing independently for short periods of time, sharing toys and playing nicely with other children. The more life skills that you teach your children, the more self-sufficient, independent and capable they become.

It is a process, of course. When they were tiny, we did everything for them. As they grow, we begin to help them learn to do it for themselves. We do supervise to make sure they do it correctly. With time and practice, eventually they get to a point where they're capable of being able to do it well themselves.

IN THIS CHAPTER

- ◆ **Chores**
- ◆ **Teeth-brushing battles**
- ◆ **Faddy dressing**
- ◆ **Haircut fights**
- ◆ **Getting used to dogs**
- ◆ **Learning to play alone**
- ◆ **Play groups and play dates**
- ◆ **Healthy boundaries**
- ◆ **Stretching attention span**
- ◆ **Overcoming frustration**
- ◆ **Lying**
- ◆ **Dealing with disappointment**

If parents don't teach life skills, a child becomes arrested in their development. It's as if they are still in the baby stage.

Parents often wonder how and when to teach these things, which are the questions I address in this chapter. Plus I help you deal with common toddler issues around these skills, like faddy dressing and resisting haircuts. The social skills can be particularly challenging – how do I help my child get along well with others? What if he's shy? Aggressive? What do I do if my child gets frustrated easily? Has trouble handling disappointment? All my answers are here.

When to Start Chores

Q *I have to confess that my parents never made me do chores. I now know that wasn't perhaps the best thing to do as I had a lot of rude awakenings as a young adult as to how to be on my own. So I want to do it differently with my kids. But I have no idea of what to have them do and when to start. I have a two-year-old and an almost five-year-old.*

A I'm often asked when is a good time to start giving children household chores and what, exactly, is age-appropriate. Chores are one of the ways kids learn life skills. However, toddlers shouldn't have set chores – they're too young. And you can't expect a two- or three-year-old to do things on their own without being instructed and supervised over and over. You must show them how to put their toys away, one step at a time, and how to wipe up a spill.

One of the best ways to get them to learn is through the Mother's Little Helper technique (see box on page 118), where they do things with you, rather than you making them do it on their own. Toddlers want to do things with you and they want to help. Make it fun and they will enjoy chores.

What chores are appropriate for each age? Here are my suggestions:

Two to three

- ◆ **Put toys away.**
- ◆ **Pick up puzzles and put books back on the shelf.**
- ◆ **Put clothes in the laundry basket.**
- ◆ **Put nappy in the bin.**
- ◆ **Help tidy up arts and crafts.**
- ◆ **Put bath toys away.**

As you can see, most of these little chores are about putting things away and learning where things go. This teaches them to tidy and look after their things.

Four to five

- **Any of the above chores, plus:**
- **Make own bed or at least attempt to. Let's face it; it's a duvet these days.**
- **Help clear the table, for example, bringing plastic cups into the kitchen.**
- **Wipe up spills.**
- **Use hand-held vacuum or dustpan and brush to pick up crumbs. (Kids love this one!)**
- **Water the plants and feed the fish (with help – they love this one so much they can overdo it!)**
- **Wash picnicware at the sink.**
- **Pour cereal into bowl.**
- **Put away coat and shoes.**
- **Help load the washing machine with Mummy.**
- **Match socks up and identify their own clothes in a pile.**

As you can see, I use the word chores very flippantly here, because having our toddlers help us with the little things of everyday life helps them learn the importance of doing little things as a family.

THE MOTHER'S LITTLE HELPER TECHNIQUE

- **Get them involved in whatever you're doing: carrying items at the grocery shop, clearing the table, sweeping the floor. Of course it will take longer, but you will be interacting with one another and teaching them important skills.**
- **Make a badge that says 'Mother's Little Helper'. Tell them they will get the badge when they finish helping.**
- **Be sure to tell them what a good job they're doing in helping you.**

Teeth-Brushing

Q *Help! I fight with my three-year-old to brush her teeth. She wants to do it herself, which, of course, she can't do adequately. What should I do?*

A I know it can be annoying and time-consuming when your toddler insists on 'Me do!' but it is actually a good sign that she is moving on in her development. However, to make sure your child's teeth are properly cared for, you can't leave her to do it on her own until she's about seven because it is only then that she has the dexterity to do it properly. Let her do it first and praise her for her effort. Then say, 'Great! Now it's Mummy's turn.' As you brush her teeth, talk her through each step so eventually she will learn the proper technique. See the box below.

PROPER TEETH-BRUSHING

- **Use a pea-sized dab of fluoride toothpaste.**

- **Use a soft-bristled toothbrush and brush gently back and forth. Start with the inside surface first, where plaque may accumulate most.**

- **Clean the outer surfaces of each tooth. Angle the brush along the outer gum line at 90 degrees to the teeth.**

- **Brush the chewing surface of each tooth.**

- **While you brush, sing, sing, sing or use a timer. You want to spend at least a couple of minutes brushing your children's teeth, as I believe it is something they should see takes time to do properly so that good oral hygiene is maintained.**

Dressing

Q *My three-and-a-half-year-old insists on dressing herself and wearing her pink tutu every single day, everywhere, no matter how inappropriate.*

A While I approve of toddlers dressing up as part of their pretend play, it sounds like you might have a faddy dresser. This is when a child becomes fixated on a particular item. I believe in nipping that behaviour in the bud or it can go on for months. The night before, lay out a different outfit. In the morning, offer plenty of positive encouragement when she puts it on without a battle of the wills. Set times for when she can wear her dressing-up clothes. That way she can get fully engrossed in her make-believe wardrobe as well as her normal clothes.

Haircut Fights

Q *How do I get my three-year-old son to allow us to cut his hair again? It was never an issue, but all of a sudden he throws such a tantrum and seems terrified. We've used both the clippers and shears. He doesn't like either any more. He runs away, cries, screams, kicks. We've tried distracting him with cartoons and rewarding him, but nothing works.*

A I think the shears' vibration might be causing concern on his head. He might be hearing the buzz. I suggest you go back to a hairdresser. Here are my step-by-step suggestions:

◆ **Be more nonchalant in your attitude. It has to seem to your little boy that it is something that everyone does and it is no big deal.**

◆ **Let him know in advance when you are going.**

◆ **Let him know that you are going somewhere exciting afterwards; his motivation will be higher.**

* Let him choose something to bring to distract himself.

* Go when it is less busy.

* Hang back and let the hairdresser deal with him unless he asks for you.

* Praise your child for his efforts.

Getting Used to Dogs

(Q) *My toddler is afraid of dogs. She screams and runs away any time she sees one. How can I help her get comfortable? Her grandmother has a Golden Retriever and I want her to be able to be in the same room with him!*

(A) Being afraid of dogs is not uncommon. Their barks are loud, they move quickly and unpredictably, and even medium-sized ones can knock a toddler over. Such fear often goes away as your child gets older, but you can take measures to make her more comfortable. Exposure over and over again does help, if you do it right:

* Help her overcome her fear in small steps. Have her stroke a small puppy, first with your hand shadowing over hers, on several occasions. Then graduate to a very calm, well-behaved dog that you can count on to not jump up or bark.

* When she is feeling comfortable doing this with you, have her stroke it by herself.

* Each time you expose her, model patting the dog and offer reassurance so she sees for herself that it is possible to have a nice experience even if it's after a few tries.

* Having her in the same room as the dog but by your side will allow her to observe the dog in natural surroundings with the reassurance of you next to her. As she becomes more confident she will have less fear.

* In parks, know that any dog running towards you is going to be scary for any little toddler. So pick her up and let her see it from your height.

If the dog comes to your feet and calms down, you can then place her down slowly, patting the dog as she does so too.

Playing Alone

Q *I am a stay-at-home mum who can't get a thing done because my three-year-old clings to my side every second of every waking hour. I can't get her to stay in a room by herself long enough for me even to do dishes. She goes to nursery two days a week for one and a half hours a day. I am seriously thinking of putting her in full-time, so I can have time to myself and get some housework done. Are there any other solutions?*

A I think the issue here is that you haven't helped your daughter learn *how* to play alone and more time in nursery won't help her with that, although it will help her with socialization and you with housework. Playing independently is not something you can expect a child to figure out on her own. You can't just hand her a toy and say, 'Go in the other room and play.' To help her learn, I suggest you use the Play and Stay, Play Away technique (see box opposite.) Typically you would do this when she was a bit younger, but you can certainly do it now. I would suggest working up to ten minutes or so alone, always making sure you're supervising so that you know she's safe. I would also encourage you to have company around so that she can get used to playing without you having to be the one that she plays with all the time. It's equally important that when you are with her you are interacting. If she feels like she isn't getting any attention from you because you are always busy doing household chores, she will cling to you even more.

THE PLAY AND STAY, PLAY AWAY TECHNIQUE

- Play with her for a bit with something she enjoys doing, like a puzzle she knows or making a tower of blocks. Then say, 'Mummy's going to the kitchen, I'll be back in a minute.'

- Walk out of the room and then come back in a couple of minutes. You don't want to leave your child unattended for a long period of time. This is just to show her that you may go into another room, but you always come back.

- Do this at various times throughout the day so she'll learn through the repetition that you always come back.

Help with Happier Play Groups

Q *My three friends and I decided to form a play group with our four three-year-olds. No matter whose house it's at, all we seem to do is referee toy-snatching and investigate why someone is crying. Can you help us have a happy play group?*

A Play groups provide an opportunity for toddlers to develop social skills – learning how to play with others, to share and co-operate. Here are my tips for a happy play group:

- Keep the time short – no more than 90 minutes, two hours max.

- The best time to do it is in the morning after breakfast and long before nap time, so your children are rested, fed and ready to play.

- Plan a few short, structured activities, like play dough, puzzles or colouring together, as well as having unstructured play time. It doesn't have to be fancy. At this age they can't be just left to play with each other. They need help figuring out what to do.

- The four of you must closely supervise when your toddlers are together. Treat the group as an opportunity to teach your child proper behaviour, rather than seeing it as a problem when there's a set-to. Expect issues and plan for them. Agree that each mum will deal with her own child and create group rules: no grabbing toys, no hitting, etc. Keep them short and simple, three max.

- Explain the rules to the children and explain that if the rules are not followed, there will be a warning and if the warning is not heeded, that person will have to sit out.

- Sometimes your child is not being aggressive towards another child, but he's hoarding toys or not playing fairly. Then I'd use the Sideline technique (see box on page 127).

Because your children are just learning to socialise, you may see certain behaviours like hanging back and not engaging, bullying, grabbing toys, hitting or biting. Play groups also raise the issue of how you deal with misbehaviour of other people's children. Here are my suggestions for these issues:

Shyness

If your child shows tendencies not to get immediately involved with the toys or the other children, let him watch the other toddlers play. Then, at some stage, you need to coax him away from your side and out to play. Guide him over to where other children are playing and help him get involved with a toy. Show him what fun he can have at the sand pit or the water table alongside the other children. Let him know that you're watching. He'll begin to enjoy it and eventually won't need coaxing. But understand that it's not until four, five and beyond that you start to see kids really playing with each other. Before that, they play next to one another.

Sharing

Before you leave home, make the expectations clear in advance and explain in very simple language what sharing is: 'We're going to the play group. We're going to be sharing the toys and that means that all of the toys will be for everybody to have their turn. It will be your turn and then it will be somebody else's turn.' If she has trouble sharing during the play group, your response should be moderate – it's nothing to over-react about. Just say, 'You need to share.' Some children have trouble sharing space. They're on a bouncy castle or the ball pool and they don't want anyone else in it. Then you need to explain: 'Sharing means other people can come in. It means we *all* play with it.' If your child grabs a toy from someone, say, 'He was playing with it first. And then it will be your turn.' Practise the Taking Turns technique at home (see page 97).

Spitting, Hitting, Biting

None of these are acceptable and must be dealt with straight away, using the Spit, Bit, Hit technique (see page 90).

Bullying

If you see your child intimidating or bullying others, you need to deal with it straight away, using the Sideline technique (page 127) or the Naughty Step. I would also suggest apologising to the parent of the other child. Then you need to work on his sharing skills (see Taking Turns technique, page 97) and social skills so that he doesn't feel like he has to intimidate others. This is incredibly important to do in the toddler years. Parents need to deal with this head on rather than laugh it off or justify it. You *have* to be responsible for your child's behaviour. Your child is not going to be responsible for his behaviour because he's just *learning* how to behave.

Telling off Someone Else's Child

As a parent, you *cannot* tell somebody else's child off or implement any form of discipline unless you have permission to do it. That's not your responsibility.

What you *can* do is, for instance, if you see another child smack yours, go over and attend to your child. If the other child is standing there, you can say, 'That wasn't nice at all. You really hurt her.' In other words, you can make her aware of what she's done, but discipline is the parent's responsibility. That's why it is so important for all parents to step up and deal with their children's misbehaviour. What's frustrating for a lot of parents is when other parents turn a blind eye to what their child has done. Everybody talks about it behind closed doors and nobody says it at the time because they are afraid of confrontation. But *know* that when your child hits someone, the parent is looking for you to put it right! And when you don't, they think, 'I can't believe that that parent didn't *even* tell his child off for what they just did.'

PLAY DATES

My advice for play dates would be similar to play groups, although often in this circumstance you might be alone with your child and his friend. Then I would let the parent know your rules and your discipline approach and get her permission to apply those rules to her child if necessary. When I was in that situation, I would always let a parent know if her child ended up on the Naughty Spot so that she isn't hearing it for the first time from the toddler at home later.

THE SIDELINE TECHNIQUE

- ◆ **Remind him to share what he has.**

- ◆ **If he doesn't, pick him up and place him on the sideline of the activity so he can see everybody else getting along and having fun.**

- ◆ **Say, 'You know what? You didn't play fairly, so now you've got to sit out for a little while and then you can go back and join in.'**

- ◆ **Keep him out for a couple of minutes, just long enough for him to get the point, 'If you want to play, you have to play fairly.'**

Learning Boundaries

Q My three-and-a-half-year-old constantly interrupts when I am on the phone or when a friend of mine is over. She lies on top of me, pulls on me and generally acts up. Is this jealousy and what can I do about it?

A This is absolutely natural and common to all toddlers. A toddler wants all of you. She wants your food, your attention, your body, your bed. Starting around two, your child needs to learn healthy boundaries by you teaching her not to invade your space. Have her sit next to you rather than on your lap. Put her back in her own bed when she migrates to yours. Insist she eats her food before she can have something on your plate. Teach her to say 'Excuse me' when you are in a conversation. At this age, she can't be expected to wait silently for a long amount of time, but she can learn to say 'Excuse me' before you respond to her. From about four years old onwards, you should ask her to wait a bit. Start with a short time: 'Mum, look at this!' 'Wait a minute! Mummy's saying goodbye.' Then give your attention. The older she gets, the more you can increase the amount of waiting time. Everybody has an invisible parameter of space and for healthy relationships we need to learn boundaries that we reside within. This is certainly a life skill that needs to be taught constantly, so repetition is critical.

Stretching Attention Span

Q I just got some upsetting feedback from my daughter's nursery. They said she is really having trouble sitting still and focusing on an activity. Now I am worried she has ADD. What can I do?

A First of all, no parent likes to hear anything about their child that could be taken as being negative. But I would encourage you to look at feedback from nursery teachers as an indication of how you can support your child in ensuring a positive experience at school. Before jumping to the conclusion that she has ADD, I would encourage you to consider whether she needs help at home in learning the life skill of attention. Children are not born with long attention spans. You have to train a child's concentration. I think what the teachers are saying to you is that in addition to what they are doing at school, you should spend some time each day helping her learn to focus. Here are some ways:

♦ **Pick an activity that is challenging to her but not beyond her abilities, like a puzzle. Sit down with her and encourage her to do it. If she starts to walk away before she's done or move onto something else, coax her back: 'Come on, we're not finished.' You may have to help her re-engage: 'You could put that piece there.' When she does it, make sure you praise her: 'Look at that, you did it! I am proud of you for finishing.'**

♦ **Read her a book and engage her if she starts to wander off: 'Sit down and let's find out what happens to the bunny! What do you think happens? Can you turn the page for me?' Choose highly interactive books that give her things to pull, touch and open to engage her even more.**

♦ **Once you've increased her attention a bit, work on her sticking to something without you. Start her off with something interesting and then go away for a minute. When you return, if she's moved on to something else, bring her back to the first activity.**

As you work with her, you should see her capacity to engage by herself increase over time. Check in with the nursery after a month or so to see how it's going there as well. If they – and/or you – are still concerned, talk to your doctor.

Overcoming Frustration

Q *I'm a mother who is an artist. I love to sit down and do arts and crafts with my son. He gets so frustrated when he cannot do something by himself. How do I help him to get through this?*

A It's wonderful that, as an artist and a mother, you recognise the importance of creative time with your son. You're going to need a lot of perseverance. It's quite natural for a toddler to know in his mind what he wants to achieve and get frustrated, to say the least, when he doesn't have the fine motor skills to do it. You need to be comfortable with him trying it himself, getting frustrated, and then coming through the other end. Every now and then, ask if he needs your help. If he gets annoyed when you ask him or says no but can't work it out himself, sit next to him and do it yourself without saying anything. Sometimes children will look over at what *you're* doing and then attempt it themselves. But adversity is good. It teaches him to have more patience, to slow down, to concentrate and focus and then finally to get it, if not this time, then certainly with practice.

Teaching Child to Tell the Truth

Q *I'm the mother of a five-year-old who is very articulate and smart. She recently lied to me and continued to lie to me, even when I told her I knew the truth. How do I raise my daughter to tell the truth?*

A Children under the age of five generally don't consciously lie. They are reading the people around them and how others are responding to what's happening. They just go with the flow without a real kind of conscious understanding. And very young toddlers can get mixed up in their 'no's and 'yes'es. You ask if they've gone poo and they say 'no' even when they have. From the age of five or six, however, children become more consciously aware of what they're saying and the impact that it has on others. That's when you home in on character-building so that they start to become very honest in telling you the truth.

Your smart and articulate five-year-old is aware that, if she told you the truth, she could get in trouble. That's why kids lie. In order to help build her character, what's most important in this situation is that your child feels good about being honest and open with you and that you help her to learn that it makes her a better person to tell the truth about a situation.

That's why I always tell parents that if you shout at kids or convey anger when you ask them whether they're lying to you, a very smart child is going to learn to lie very quickly. If you think your child is lying, you need to be quite matter-of-fact: 'Let's find out what happened here. Talk to me about what *really* happened because Mummy wants to help you.' Then they are more open to a conversation that allows you to get to the bottom of what's going on and resolve it. This helps your child recognise what she can do better next time.

If the behaviour being covered up with a lie warrants a consequence, then you can still go ahead and give one. For instance, 'I'm glad that you told the truth because Mummy always wants you to be honest. But the thing you did, you do know that that's naughty and for that you need to go on the Naughty Step.' Then your child will learn to recognise that you're being fair but still opening your relationship for her to be honest with you.

You'll find that if you can begin this very early on, when your child is a teenager she will feel comfortable coming to you and saying, 'I made a really big mistake. I've come to you because you are my parent and I need help in resolving it.' She won't be afraid to come to you for help. What we want to do is help our children over time learn to be accountable for their behaviour and admit their mistakes. Because mistakes are part and parcel of growing up.

Dealing with Disappointment

Q *How can I help my child deal with surprise or disappointment? When he loses a game or drops a ball, or if something unexpected happens during his day – good or bad – my toddler just can't seem to cope and gets very upset and unsettled.*

A You have to teach good sportsmanship, how to be a good loser, and the spirit of enjoying the game – win or lose. You can help him learn by talking about the experience as you're doing it: 'This is fun, isn't it? We're enjoying ourselves, aren't we?' Does it stop the fact that a toddler will get disappointed when he loses and smash all the pieces on the board? No, it doesn't. That comes with time. But you help him understand the process: 'When we play this, we get to here. When we get here, that makes somebody the winner. When someone wins, we say, "Well done. Good job. You won that game. Do you want to play another?"' And of course you don't ever want to ridicule a child for losing – then it's going to be seen as a bad thing to experience.

While it's important to teach good sportsmanship, I don't think you want to stop him feeling surprised or disappointed. It's important for children to have those emotions. If you're disappointed that you ran a race and you didn't win, then you know what? You are going to try harder. I feel strongly about parents attempting to shelter their children from feeling disappointment or hurt. Adversity makes us do better. It brings out more of our potential.

Part of what you need to help your child do is learn to adapt to disappointment. Otherwise, you're just setting him up for a warped sense of life. You can help your child adapt through your response. If he drops a ball, you can say, 'Never mind, pick it up!' Or if he falls off his bike: 'All right, let's get back on it again!' If it's no big deal for you, then it will not be such a big deal for him.

8

Out and About

Getting out of the house and going places with toddlers is important. It helps them learn how to behave in public and feel comfortable in new surroundings. It exposes them to new places and experiences. And it's just plain fun for you and them – how delightful is it to see something like an elephant at the zoo for the first time through your child's eyes? Or enjoy a walk in the park together on a sunny spring day?

But going out and about with a toddler can also be challenging. All the issues you are dealing with at home – tantrums, pushing for independence, learning to sit at the table – go along with you, but now you are in public for the world to see! That's why parents often shy away from taking their toddlers out to restaurants or the shops, or on holiday. They don't want the car seat fight, the tantrum in the sweets aisle. But avoiding these situations is just that – avoidance. It doesn't help you teach your child proper behaviour in public and it cuts you and her off from the chance to enjoy a whole wide variety of experiences.

You want the pleasure of being able to go out and about with your kids – to explore what's beyond your front door. The reality is that nobody wants to be cooped up inside their home with cabin fever. But in order to be able to enjoy all of what is available beyond our front door – from music classes to library reading groups to meals out with friends – we've got to make sure that our children listen to us so they stay safe and know how to behave in social situations.

Going out with toddlers – whether around the corner or halfway across the world –can be fun for all of you when you are prepared and armed with the proper information. That's what this section is all about: ensuring that your adventures outside the house are as carefree and enjoyable as possible. I tackle parents' most pressing issues, such as car seat battles and siblings squabbling in the car, making sure your child sticks by you while walking, doing errands together, dealing with problems at the playground, staying cool in hot weather, and tips for having a wonderful family holiday. *Bon voyage!*

IN THIS CHAPTER

◆ **Car squabbles and car seat resistance**

◆ **Running away**

◆ **Reins**

◆ **Doing errands**

◆ **Playground etiquette**

◆ **Staying cool in hot weather**

◆ **Family holidays**

Squabbling in the Car

 Between errands, toddler activities and school drop-off and pick-up for the oldest, I feel like my three kids (two, three and five) and I spend our lives in the car. I can tell they get bored because they start fighting with one another – poking, arguing, grabbing. How can I make this easier on me – and them?

A As the driver your first priority is safety. You need to be in control at all times. Here are my suggestions for trouble-free car travel around town:

♦ **Make a box with toys and car games and put it where they can get at it themselves. Rotate the items in it every few weeks.**

♦ **If travel coincides with snack time, make sure you have snacks with you – juice boxes, cheese sticks, cut-up fruit. A hungry traveller is a crabby one.**

♦ **Put together an emergency kit: first aid kit; two-litre bottle of water; wipes, pre-paid phone card; dried fruit; crackers; mini-flashlight.**

♦ **No over-the-shoulder discipline. Stop the car on a hard shoulder or a parking space when your kids act up and give a warning straight away. Don't wait till they've gone absolutely mad. Explain to them that your safety is important so you need to concentrate on driving. If they don't listen, give consequences and follow through.**

♦ **Carry a mat to use as a Naughty Spot if needed.**

♦ **If your kids are constantly fighting in the car, do a car drill. (See box on page 136)**

CAR DRILLS

- ◆ **Write up a sheet with the car rules: 1. One game or toy; 2. Seat belts and car seats; 3. House rules in car – respect, take turns, no hitting or yelling.**
- ◆ **Go over the rules.**
- ◆ **Call out 'car drill' and have them practise getting into the car and strapping themselves in. Help little ones.**
- ◆ **Pretend to take a trip as they play in the back.**

Car Seat Fights

Q *I can't get my two-and-a-half-year-old into his car seat. Sometimes he's a gem, other times he screams and kicks. I try to stay calm, but some days it's really hard.*

A Right now, your son is seeking control and doesn't realise the necessity of car seats. Step one is to role-play being in the car seat at home. Make it a fun game. Sit on cushions in the living room, on his bed, or in a big cut-up cardboard box. Bring his car seat in and get him used to sitting in it when he otherwise wouldn't have to, and help him learn to strap himself in. Make it as real as possible – don't forget to open the car door, put on a seat belt and 'drive' the car on an adventure.

Next, try it in the car. There's no point in yelling. Car seats and seat belts are mandatory and have to be got into and done up without a struggle. It is the way of the world. When he sees you becoming more relaxed and getting the job done, he won't escalate either.

More Car Seat Fighting

Q *My son hates getting in the car and fights me every time I try to put him into his car seat. Sometimes this can be quite dangerous. Sometimes he crawls between the front and back seats so I can't get at him. It's like a cat and mouse game. Can you give me some techniques to make this a whole lot easier?*

A Your child obviously is being very defiant and not listening to anything you say. This is, as you say, a dangerous situation. A child who doesn't listen to you when it's about car safety is the same child that will run across the road! He doesn't respect your authority so everything you say is going in one ear and out the other. That's the cycle that needs to stop, because it's not just happening in the car. I certainly know from doing *Supernanny* and *Extreme Parental Guidance* that behaviour like this outside the home means there's not enough discipline in the home either.

His learning to take instruction and do as he's told is *incredibly* important here. You have to establish your authority:

◆ **Set expectations clearly in advance, before you get in the car. Crouch down about two feet in front of him, face to face, and make eye contact.**

◆ **Speak in a low, slow voice and explain what is expected: 'You are going to get in the car seat now and wear your seat belt.'**

- ◆ **Explain the consequences for not listening: 'If you don't get into your seat right now you will go on the Naughty Spot. If I see for any moment that you have taken your seat belt off while we are in the car, I will be pulling the car over and, trust me, you're going to be in trouble. You will go on the Naughty Spot when we get home.'**

- ◆ **If he doesn't do as you say, you** *have* **to follow through on consequences or else he'll never take you seriously. You have to nip this behaviour straight in the bud. The fact that you play cat and mouse means that he's got into the cycle of grabbing your attention through not listening to you.**

- ◆ **Read the Discipline chapter in this book and make sure you are putting boundaries, warnings and consequences in place at home as well. Look particularly at page 29 on voice tone and eye contact. He must learn to respect your authority.**

Running Away

Q *My three-year-old runs away* **every time** *I take him shopping or out for the day. It's getting dangerous now and he's getting too big for the shopping trolley. How can I discipline him and keep control when out and about?*

A Running away is a dangerous situation for you as it is potentially lethal with traffic everywhere. As he is three, he needs to learn to listen and do as he is told. So, firstly, your authority needs to be respected. See my bulleted suggestions in the previous question. Secondly, if he is always in a shopping trolley or a stroller, he is going to feel tied down and so when the opportunity presents itself he will *run*! Please use my Roaming technique (see box opposite). This will give him the independence to roam but to be safe at the same time.

THE ROAMING TECHNIQUE PART I

◆ When he wants to walk, give a clear choice between two options: hold your hand and walk or hold onto the stroller. What he can't do is walk by himself.

◆ If he refuses to obey, then he has to be in the stroller.

THE ROAMING TECHNIQUE PART II

◆ Use the Roaming Technique Part II for children between three and five years:

◆ Practise in a quiet, car-free place, like a park or shop. You want the environment to be safe as he learns the basics.

◆ Explain that you are going to let him out of the stroller or trolley, but when you say 'Stop' and hold up your hand, he needs to stop wherever he is.

◆ Say, 'Now you can get out!' and help him out.

◆ The first few times, have him walk just ahead of you and then say 'Stop'. If he doesn't stop, have him hold your hand or the stroller or trolley for a few minutes. If he does wait for you, praise him and then let him go again.

◆ When you say 'Stop' use a low, authoritative tone of voice.

◆ Work up to allowing him to go a bit further, explaining that Mummy or Daddy always needs to see him, so he can't run off too far.

◆ As you build up trust and he shows he can listen, let him walk further ahead. Remember, trust is built on an invisible child rein.

Not Able to Chase a Child

Q   *I am a proud grandad who has a five-year-old grandson. I recently had a knee operation and can't walk as fast as I used to. How do I take him to the park without fearing he will run away from me?*

A   Congratulations, Grandad, on your 5-year-old grandson and I hope you're having a speedy recovery from your knee operation. As one who's just had one, I know it takes a lot of perseverance!

In this situation, it's really important, first and foremost, that your grandchild learns to take direction and do as he's told. When you are confident he will listen to you, it lessens the fear. While you are recovering, however, there are things that you can do to enjoy going to the park safely. Stay in areas that you feel are safe, for instance in a gated play area where your grandson can't get out on his own. Set down the expectation that he must hold your hand until you get to a certain area – for instance, the swings, where you can then watch him. When he's ready to move on, he holds your hand again to go to the slide.

But if you're really in a place where if he did run off you wouldn't be able to catch him, make sure you go with somebody else who can run after him if necessary. The reality is that, as much as five-year-olds listen, they're still quite impulsive. If they see something interesting, they don't always see the fear or the danger that's in front of them.

Reins for Wanderers?

Q   *What are your thoughts on child restraints or leashes? My 14-month-old is full of energy. Everywhere we go she likes to venture off from me. Sometimes I feel embarrassed because I meet with other parents and their 15–18-month-old children don't leave their sides. Is this a personality thing or a problem? I am worried my child might be showing early signs of ADHD. The reason I say this is because I was diagnosed with ADHD as a child.*

A It's a parent's responsibility to make sure that their child is protected and kept safe at all times. As your child is so young, my goal would be to take her to places where she can run around and feel free. And in places where she can't, like walking on a pavement, put her into a stroller or hold her hand or pick her up. See also my Roaming techniques on page 139.

I am not opposed to child reins. There are parents who have handicaps and cannot run after their child, so leashes do have their place. However, don't use them as a substitute for teaching your child to do what she is told. What we want to do is encourage your child's listening skills. Ask her to 'Get something for Mummy' or play games like 'Simon Says'. Give her lots of repetition because she won't get the listening games right away as she's still learning basic language and grasping commands.

As an adult with ADHD, you know the importance of teaching a child to focus and interact. I would not assume, however, that your child has ADHD. It's natural at the age of 14 months to want to go, go, go. One very positive thing you can do is work on her attention span. See my answer on page 128.

Problems Running Errands with Toddler

Q *I am a stay-at-home mum who is so frustrated with trying to do errands with my four-year-old that I am seriously thinking of staying home for good. She whines and drags her feet after a very short time. Plus she wants everything she sees and throws a fit when I say no. I am at my wits' end.*

A There is no question that doing errands with a toddler can be challenging, but that doesn't mean you should avoid it. It's part of what your child needs to learn – that she can't have everything she sees. Here's how to make it go more smoothly. First, you can't be out for hours – that is just unfair on your child. You want to spend no more than 30–60 minutes before you do some child-friendly activity. Keeping it short will help prevent her having meltdowns. Mornings, right after breakfast, are the best time to go as she is well rested and fed.

Use the Involvement technique (see box on page 142) to keep up her interest in what you're doing. A bored toddler is a cranky one. Make shopping an adventure and you will have a more co-operative little one.

If you want to curb the 'I want everythings', do not buy her a treat every time you go shopping. Treats are treats, not habits. If it's not a treat day, make it clear before you go into a shop that you will not be buying anything that is not on the list. Don't say she 'may' get a treat. Don't promise a treat for 'later'. Even though you've gone over the rules, in the shop she will ask for things anyway. That's when you remind her that you told her you're not going to get anything for her today. If she has a tantrum in response, follow my suggestions for tantrums on pages 90–91. Above all, do not give in! The only way to stop her behaviour is for her to learn it doesn't pay off. Stay strong, follow through and you won't have to fight this battle forever.

THE INVOLVEMENT TECHNIQUE

- As you go through a shop, talk about items on your list. Ask her to help you find them. Have her feel the different textures, smell the different smells, identify the different colours.

- Give her a crayon and have her tick off each item on your list as you go.

Playground Etiquette

Q *I used to like to take my three-year-old to the park so he could get fresh air and run around. But recently there have been other kids there who are bullying him – snatching his toys and not letting him up on the slide. The parents just sit there and do nothing. What is the proper playground etiquette in those situations? Is it right to step in and reprimand another person's child? We don't have another place to go close by.*

A This is always a touchy situation, isn't it? But it's important that your toddler gets at least one hour of physical activity a day as part of a healthy lifestyle, so you are right that you need to find a way to resolve it.

I would first suggest directly intervening with the child, but not with a reprimand. A simple 'Please take turns' at the slide or 'Please give Sam his shovel back' in a friendly tone of voice can usually easily resolve things. If this doesn't work, my advice would be to talk to the parent. Be assertive but not aggressive. Walk over to the parent and say, 'You may not have noticed, but your daughter just snatched my son's sand toy and won't give it back. These things happen with toddlers because they are just learning to share. Thanks so much.' If the mum was just not paying attention well, you alert her. If you are met with a parent who doesn't choose to act upon the information given then unfortunately there is nothing you can really do about it. This is something I hear of quite often. It is my hope that parents understand the importance of teaching their children proper manners, but I know that starts with parents having them in the first place!

I would also help your child learn what to say in these situations. Teach him to say, 'Please give me back my toy', 'Please let me go down the slide'. You can't leave him on his own to defend himself at this age, but you do want to set the stage for him being able to speak up for himself as he gets older.

Staying Cool

We're about to go on holiday to a hot climate and we want to make sure our 18-month-old, who is very mobile, doesn't get burnt or sick from the heat. What can we do?

To keep a child cool, I like to wet a face towel and freeze it. When it's nice and cold but not rock solid, put it around your child's neck and at her pulse points. Monitor your child's outdoor time. Go outside early or late in the day, not midday, and limit the time outside if it is very hot. If your child is over-heated, sweaty or red-faced, get her into a lukewarm bath immediately. This is the fastest way to bring down her body temperature. Watch for signs of heat exhaustion or the much more dangerous heat stroke. (See box on page 144.)

Appetites can decrease in hot weather, so don't be nervous if your toddler is eating less. Just make sure you have more snacks available. Remember to keep her hydrated. You can monitor your child's hydration by taking a look at her urine. It should be essentially colourless. If it's very yellow or darkish, that means she's not well hydrated. Keep an eye on your child's nappy as well; if it's not as wet as it normally is, she's not drinking enough. Pedialyte and Dioralyte are common fluids used for diarrhoea, but it doesn't hurt to put some in the drink of an over-heated child, as they have electrolytes in them.

HEAT STROKE AND HEAT EXHAUSTION

Heat stroke is a life-threatening condition that occurs when the body's temperature rises and its ability to cool down shuts off. Toddlers are especially vulnerable, so you'll need to keep a close eye on holidays to warm climates. Severe sunburn can also bring on heat stroke. Heat stroke can occur in mere minutes if you leave your toddler in a parked car as the temperature inside climbs much higher and faster than outside. That's why you can never leave a child in a hot car for even a minute.

Symptoms of heat stroke include a temperature of 39.4°C (103°F) or higher, with no sweating; hot, red, dry skin and rapid pulse; rapid, shallow breathing; restlessness, confusion; dizziness, headache or vomiting; lethargy (for instance, not responding as strongly as usual when you call his name or tickle him); unconsciousness. **If you see any of these symptoms, call 999 (or if abroad, be sure to know that emergency number) and work to bring his internal temperature down as fast as possible while you are waiting for the ambulance**. Undress your toddler completely and lay him down in a cool room or in the shade if you can't get to a room. Sponge down his body with a flannel dipped in cool water, and fan him with a magazine or an electric fan.

Heat exhaustion symptoms include: thirst, fatigue, cool, moist skin and leg or stomach cramps. Bring him indoors to an air-conditioned room if possible, and offer plenty of liquids. Avoid drinks that are very sugary or cold, as these can cause stomach cramps. Give him a cool bath or shower and keep him indoors for the rest of the day. If he doesn't seem to be improving quickly, take him to your GP or local hospital.

Wear loose-fitting, lightweight and lightly coloured clothes rather than dark ones, which absorb more heat. To make sure she is protected from the sun, dress her in shirts or dresses with long sleeves. I love UV-ray-protective clothing because it gives greater peace of mind, especially when out in the water. Wetsuit tops are also good. Protect her head with hats that have peak and tails. Don't forget UV-protected sunglasses.

And please do not forget sunscreen protection. As we know, in some countries this is becoming an expensive purchase; but it should be used every couple of hours and NOT in moderation. Even when the sky is overcast, UV is still penetrating, so do not be fooled by the lack of sun and make sure you lotion-up. Apply it before putting on protective clothing. Lead by example and do this as much for yourself as you do for your kids. See my suggestions for putting sunscreen on toddlers on page 81.

First Family Holiday

Q *I am about to take that first family holiday with my one-and-a-half- and three-year-olds. What can I do to maximise the fun and minimise the hassle? I'm already stressing out over all the equipment I must bring – car seats, stroller, pack and play, etc.*

A Travelling successfully with children is all about preparation and organisation. The more you plan in advance, the happier you will all be. Take into account the pros and cons of the different modes of transport: car journeys allow you to pile all their equipment in the boot, as well as stop along the way to give the kids breaks. With planes, the journey may be quicker, but there's no getting off, and carrying around a tote bag will make it easier. Trains are different because they allow for more mobility with kids. Plus the sleeping cabins are wonderful and adventurous for the young!

Once you've decided on location and type of transportation, work out when it's best to go – during the night, so they can sleep on the way? Early enough, so they're not tired all day? Lots of parents of toddlers swear by the night car trip – the upside is they tend to sleep the whole way, the downside is that you arrived absolutely knackered while they're raring to go. If you have a partner, he or she can do the driving while you sleep and then you can take the a.m. shift upon arrival while he gets some rest. Once you've travelled with your kids somewhere relatively far, you'll know which works best for you and them.

MOTION SICKNESS

- ◆ **To prevent it beforehand, feed your toddler lightly before travelling and during the journey. Eating or drinking heavily can increase the likelihood of motion sickness. In particular, fatty foods and fizzy drinks seem to upset the stomach.**
- ◆ **Frequent, little snacks are good – and I mean little.**
- ◆ **Make sure the temperature is not too hot or cold inside the car.**
- ◆ **Take frequent breaks.**
- ◆ **Make sure the child is not bundled up in too many layers.**
- ◆ **If you find watching videos or looking at books makes it worse, have him stop.**
- ◆ **Carry paper bags for sickness and a change of clothes, just in case.**
- ◆ **If your efforts fail and your child is sick, be sure to replace lost fluids with frequent small sips of cold, still water.**

Start with a checklist of everything you must bring and tick it off as you pack to make sure things aren't forgotten. For the car, train or plane trip, pack a backpack for each child with comfort items such as a favourite stuffed animal, blanket or pillow, a book or two specifically for the journey, music, toys and games to play with, plus a few fun games they might want to play if they have an iPad. Pack a few surprises, maybe a new book or game, in your own carry-on as well for when boredom sets in. Pound shops have all kinds of items – sticker books, colouring books, Etch-a-sketch, tiny play dough containers – which makes stocking up a bit cheaper. Load up your iPod or iPad with kiddie music or download it off the Internet and burn it onto a disc for the car. Books on tape are good too, as are toddler TV shows if you have an iPad or DVD player. Be sure to use over-the-ear headphones rather than inside-the-ear ones to protect the ear more.

Pack snacks in advance in individual snack bags (remember, they are snacks and not meant to replace a meal, so do keep them small). Have a mix of healthy stuff and a few treats. And don't forget to keep your kids hydrated with water.

In a car, I always have a box with water, towels, tissues, snacks and lots of wipes just in case we're stuck on the M25. And don't forget a travel first aid kit. If your three-year-old is potty-trained, consider carrying a travel potty. Whatever you do, if he's trained, do not put him back in nappies for the trip. This confuses him and often causes regression. Bring a change of clothes in case of accidents and dress them in layers so that they can adapt to changes in temperature.

With kids this age, you can get toy tidies that you put on the back of the seats. It stops them dropping things on the floor all the time.

Pay attention to how much time you spend in the car. If you're driving six hours one day, it might be hard to get him in his car seat for another six hours' drive the next. Look for ways to break up the trip. Can you stay in one place for a day or two along the way? Minimally you want to break up long car rides with breaks to stretch your legs and get some fresh air. And remember, 'Are we there yet, Mum?' is something all kids say within 12 minutes of being in the car!

9

Potty-Training

Potty-training: it's the end of an era, right? You don't have to be changing nappies all the time. Financially, you'll be a bit better off because you do not have to lay out money every week for nappies. It's certainly the milestone that defines a toddler going into her mature toddler years.

Parents typically have lots of questions: what are the first signs to look out for, when to start, when to expect a child to remain dry through the night, what to do if peeing works but pooing is becoming problematic – the list goes on and on . . . Quite frankly, for thousands of parents, it just sometimes feels like they will never get the hang of it! I've seen parents angry, frustrated and defeated over this issue. I promise you that it does always sort itself out. It just requires perseverance, focus and support on your behalf.

Potty-training is challenging because you are not in control of it. Your child is ready when she's ready, there's not a magical age to begin. And she will decide when she pees and poos, not you. To potty-train effectively you have to let go of trying to be in control and look at what you *can* do. You can wait till you see the readiness signs. You can pay attention to how much fluid she's had. You can look for her pee and pooing patterns so you know when to prompt. You can encourage her to *want* to do it.

Ultimately I want to encourage you to have a positive attitude. Because so many people talk about how troublesome it is, many parents make a huge mountain out of a molehill. If your approach is that it's going to be problematic, then it becomes a bigger problem than it really is. Rather than thinking it's going to be dreadful, have a 'We're going to get it done' mindset. Schedule a week where you do nothing but potty-train and make up your mind that you're going to do it. Then, even if all hell freezes over, don't give up. Because if you start and then stop midway, it's that much harder later. Tell your friends, 'You're going to have to come to me.' Think before you commit to any outside activities: 'The park? We can do the park. That will be only half an hour. But we won't be going to the farm this week. That's an hour to get there and another hour.' Use my painless potty-training technique and get it done! It really does work – people on Twitter tell me every day that when they follow my steps, it works. Hopefully my answers in this section will make it easier for you and your child as well. Oh! And by the way, it isn't only boys who have trouble with the pooing, even though from the questions it may seem that way!

Signs of Potty-Training Readiness

 I'm a first-time mum and really don't know how soon I can potty-train my 18-month-old daughter.

Good on you for asking. Many parents feel under pressure to do it by a certain age so their toddler can go to nursery or 'before the new baby comes' so they won't have two in nappies. But trying to train before they are ready creates an uphill battle. You can't force it. They are ready when they are ready. At two years old, some toddlers have made the connection between wanting to go and knowing how to. However, for others that understanding doesn't kick in until later.

Here's all of what is involved before children can successfully be trained. They need bladder control, which typically begins to develop around 18 months. They also need their brain receptors to mature enough to tell them that they have to go, which begins around two. They also need the cognitive skills to picture the goal – go potty – and follow through without getting distracted. They need the co-ordination to pull their clothes up and down, and they need to understand and speak language well enough to communicate to you about the whole process! Because every child develops at a different rate, I always tell parents to look for the signs that their toddler is ready rather than focus on their age. Here are the signs that it's okay to begin potty-training:

- **Her nappy is dry when she gets up from her afternoon nap. This means she has control over her bladder.**

- **She starts talking about it: 'I've gone wee wee', 'I went poo'. That tells you she now has an awareness of the experience and perhaps is even uncomfortable in the wet or messy nappy.**

- **She can make requests: 'May I have juice?' 'Milk please', and can take instruction. It's clear she can understand what you're saying because you can have a dialogue with her. This means she has the communication abilities necessary to be trained. If not, don't start yet.**

◆ Even though you may have to wait as much as a year or longer, you can start to get her familiar with the process. Let her see you go. Explain what is going on. Show her what toilet paper is for and how to flush and wash hands after. The more normal you make it – this is what big children and adults do – the more 'normal' she will see it as a natural act.

KIT LIST FOR POTTY-TRAINING

◆ Plenty of pants/knickers.

◆ Lots of trousers that are easy to pull on and off.

◆ Potty or inner toilet seat depending on which you want to use (the seat for the regular toilet often works better for taller children who are too cramped to use a potty).

◆ Step-stool if you're using the toilet so that he can climb up (turning around and sitting down can be challenging, so he will still need your help to get on it).

◆ Travel potty.

◆ Wipes.

◆ Nappy bags to carry wet pants/knickers in if you are out and about.

◆ Bucket for soiled pants/knickers (or hand-wash and hang over the radiator or throw in the tumble dryer).

Painless Training

Q *I'm a mum with a two-and-a-half-year-old who shows all the signs he is ready to be potty-trained. But so many of my friends have had trouble training their children that I'm afraid to get started. I can feel myself avoiding it because I want to be sure to do it right. Can you help me?*

A I appreciate your honesty but I can tell you that all this will go much more smoothly if you adopt a positive attitude. Tell yourself 'It will go well' and trust yourself because you are seeing all the signs. You can't hold back from moving forward with your child because your friends have had nightmares potty-training. Please follow my suggestions so that this transition will be a smooth one for you. See my answer to the previous question; you can do this in a week or so:

◆ **Pick a week that you can concentrate on it and commit to doing it until he's got it. Stopping and starting only confuses a child and gives him the sense that he has a choice about the situation. It's your job to show him with your calm consistency that he's going to go in the potty from now on.**

◆ **Make sure, when you pick the week, that it is one that is uninterrupted. No long trips in the car, no appointments back and forth, just stay local.**

◆ **Buy two potties – one for home and a travel potty. Also buy a child's potty seat for the toilet. Some kids are afraid of the toilet or the sound of the flush, but others want to mimic Mum and Dad. Let him choose which he wants to use.**

◆ **Tell him that he's a big boy now and is ready to use the potty. Remember, a positive attitude for the transition is contagious.**

◆ **Put him in pants, not pull-ups. Here is my belief why: they're too similar to nappies and confuse the situation. I know all these brands convince us parents that pull-ups are the best way to go but, quite frankly, when you have a pull-up that goes up the same way as pants, and has the protection of a nappy, it doesn't push the child along mentally to become more aware of what's going on. The sensation of wet undies will help him learn what has just happened. Use nappies only at night as night-training comes later. Let him choose the pants – toddlers love the ones with characters on them, it makes it a fun part of the process. Also, letting him choose helps him get personally very excited about this next big stage of his development. I would say buy at least a dozen as you may go through many before he gets it. Remember, you can always hand-wash them and let them dry.**

◆ Dress him in easy-to-pull-down bottoms or, if it is warm enough in the house, let him run around in just his pants. Most toddlers love running around with nothing on anyway!

◆ Keep a mental note of the amount of fluids he's drinking so you have an accurate sense of when to prompt him. Don't not give him lots of liquids as you will dehydrate him. If it is easier to write the amount down, then do so. Also take note of his bowel movements; at this age toddlers are pretty predictable as to when they go. Normally it is twice or three times a day. As parents we look for these signs very early on. Sometimes our kids hide when they need to go for a number two. There is that deadly silence in the house and we think to ourselves . . . the house has gone really quiet . . . hmmmm . . . are they up to silent mischief? We search, only to find that they have ducked down, crouched underneath the dining table with their little faces red, taking a poo in their nappy, either confessing they have taken one when we asked them or swearing knowingly that they haven't. I remember with some children I looked after that they would take a quick shiver and I would know they had done a wee.

◆ Teach him what it feels like to need to pee. Tell him that it is an urge in his tummy down low. (You can press softly on his tummy so he feels it. Just below his belly button.)

◆ Watch over him during the day so you can see the signs he has to go. Ask him regularly, but especially first thing in the morning, after meals and nap, before leaving the house and before bed. You will need to ask A LOT: 'Do you need to go pee-pee?' 'Do you need to poo?' Accidents often happen when a toddler gets distracted, so prompt him before he gets engaged in a new activity.

◆ Remember, you may ask and they just shake their head no, so sometimes you will have to prompt by saying, 'Let's go wee-wee, you may need to go now.'

◆ If as a parent you need to urinate, sit your little one on his potty when you go. Kids become curious at this age and mimic your behaviour and associate the noise with urinating.

- When he does sit on the potty, give him space and time. A hovering, impatient parent can create too much pressure and some kids just need their space. Remember, it takes mental concentration to release that muscle that allows the body to urinate.

- When he finally pees or poos in the potty, give an abundance of praise and show facial approval but don't go seriously overboard. You have to remember he is learning a life skill that is a necessity. You don't want to find yourself caught in Tesco's forced to do this major 'potty wee wee' dance because your child is asking you to do it before he has even urinated.

- If you have decided to create a potty-training progress chart, have him put the stickers on the chart himself. I favour hanging it in the bathroom itself.

- If he does wet his pants, don't scold or shame him. This is a learning process. Firmly say, 'No we don't wee wee in our pants, we do wee wee in the potty.' To reconfirm understanding, ask, 'Where do we do wee wee?' He should say, 'Potty', and that is when you say, 'That's right! Let's make sure we do that next time.'

- Be careful with your language. Don't say, 'That's okay' every time you are met with wet or soiled underwear. It will quickly validate that it is okay for him to do this, and that confuses a child.

- Unless the underwear is soiled, do not rush to take off the wet pants. When he tells you they are wet, just note how uncomfortable it feels and make a point of saying, 'Ueee, wet pants, let's put dry ones on.' I don't believe in letting a child sit for long periods of time in wet pants, but letting him feel them wet and be uncomfortable for a few minutes will help him make the connection. Then change him and move on.

- Expose him to situations outside home. Take him and the travel potty to the park or a quick meal so he gets to practise in a variety of settings within a short car ride from home.

- Do not put him in nappies when you go over to someone else's house. Use the travel potty so that he gets the consistent message as to where he should go.

Training Twins

Q *I am trying to potty-train my boy/girl twins. Any suggestions?*

A Having twins doesn't necessarily mean potty-training them at the same time – in my experience, with twins you will find one just slightly more articulate than the other and that will normally prompt you to do that one first. It does vary by child and not necessarily by gender. Look for the signs I wrote about on page 151 to discover when each is ready.

'Let's go potty', 'Sitting on the potty', 'You want to do wee wee?', 'Let's do poo!' are all phrases as a parent of twins you will become accustomed to, so be prepared to be tired of hearing your voice! Repetition is key. And even though we want our own privacy, remember, 'monkey see, monkey do'. I would buy two potties. Even though both children may not be ready, one may decide he wants to sit and try it out when he sees the other one go. Your twins will learn a lot by observing this and other life skills in action.

Peeing Problems

Q *My daughter is great at saying 'poo poo' and off we go to do her poos in the loo, but when it comes to pee, she does it anywhere and everywhere. I leave her in her wet pants for a few minutes afterwards so she feels uncomfortable, but we can't seem to break her habit of wetting herself.*

A What's happening here is that your daughter can feel when a poo is coming. She has the warning of the churning feeling and so can let you know. But her bladder is small and when she has to pee, she feels the sensation and then bam, it's coming right then! So you have to help her know when to go for a pee. You've got to prompt her 15 or 20 minutes after her having fluids and before you go out anywhere. And when you prompt, be sure to make a statement: 'Let's go to the potty.' Don't ask her, 'Do you want to go for a pee?' Because the likely chances are she's going to want to carry on playing and she'll tell you no when she really does need to go. That's because toddlers take you literally. You've asked a question – 'Do you want to go?' – and they have answered, 'No I don't want to. I want to keep doing this.' They don't have the cognitive maturity to understand what you really mean. Especially since your child is having trouble knowing when she needs to pee, you have to be in charge of making up her mind for her: 'Time to go pee.'

Pooing in the Potty

Q *My son will be three next month and refuses to go number 2 in the potty. He's very good at letting me know when he has to go number 1 and doesn't have accidents during a nap or at night. However, we cannot get the number 2 down. If you ask him if he needs to go 'poo' he tells you no. He went number 2 a few times over the last few months in the potty and we did happy dances but he didn't stick to it. Help me please, I'm so tired of cleaning dirty underwear.*

A As frustrated as you may be, this won't go on for ever. To turn the situation around, first it's really important to take mental note of when he goes poo. There is a pattern to when kids go. some do morning, some late afternoon, and some after bath time because the warm water relaxes their muscles. There is also a pattern to how often they go. Some go once or twice a day, others more frequently, depending on the food you're giving them. So keep an eye on his history of number 2s. Understanding the pattern will help you know when to prompt him.

Keep in mind that he might actually be scared to go. If one time it may have hurt him, he may be holding in his stool. If he's holding it, you'll be able to tell because you'll now be keeping track of when he goes. Look for tell-tale signs: does he stand still? Does he turn red or hide or slightly move his bum up? These are signs you should take him to the toilet.

If he does it properly, don't do a 'happy dance'. That's making too much of a big deal of it. Praise and then move on. If he has an accident, speak to him in a firm voice and tell him: 'That's not good when you do that, you need to use the potty, we now do wee wee and poos in the potty.' Realistically, this shouldn't take you longer than a month at the most. Make sure your child is hydrated so that the colon can do its job properly. And again look out for the tell-tale signs of when he is going because that is when you need to put him straight onto the potty.

Poo Problems with New Baby

Q *My son is three and has been toilet-training for about five months. He has done very well with weeing in the toilet and is dry through the night. The trouble I have is that he refuses to do BMs in the toilet. He knows that he needs to do them, as he sneaks off and does them in private, all the while saying he doesn't need to go. We've tried rewards, time outs, crying, and ignoring it, but nothing seems to be working. It is as if he is doing it for attention or he wants to stay a baby like his brother. I'm sick and tired of reading books that state it will only take seven days to toilet-train and everyone seems to think that my son has a problem!*

A I can hear your frustration with the situation. Here's what happened: in the midst of toilet-training, his having bowel movements in the toilet has become a magnified issue. And now your intuition serves you well: yes, he is doing it for your attention, because he knows 100 per cent of your focus is dedicated to him when he doesn't behave the way you want him to. There's a big clue that you've given as to why he wants to capture your attention – a new baby. Toddlers can frequently regress or get stuck regarding potty-training when a baby arrives because it's one surefire way to get a parent's focus.

You're going to need more patience and to change your strategy. He will learn but you need to take the pressure off. Continue to praise him every time he uses the potty to urinate in, and continue to praise him when he stays dry during the night. Keep him in his underwear during the day so that when he's due to go – and by now you'll know his tell-tale signs (see my answer to the previous question if you need help with this) – very casually suggest he sits on the potty. Your unexpected casual attitude towards the circumstance will allow him to see he has no control over your emotions and therefore doing it wrong won't get him anything.

In addition, do what you can to make sure that he sees the new addition – and demands – of his baby brother have not sacrificed all of your attention. Make sure you have time alone with him. The balance of the two approaches will hopefully get you right on track.

Put Back in Nappies

Q *My three-and-a-half-year-old was trained and then all of a sudden started having accidents with number 2. I told him this was very bad and put him in nappies again. Now he refuses to poo in the potty. He waits till I put on a nappy in the evening and then he goes. What should I do?*

A The problem here is the message you gave your son by putting him back into nappies when he relapsed. What he had so proudly achieved was taken away and now he's regressed. Parents often make this mistake when they travel and then end up with training problems. Once you make the shift to pants, don't go back, even if he has an accident. That way your child gets the idea that he's past the nappy stage and must go in the potty.

Secondly, you scolded him by saying it was bad. When you scold a child, it makes him feel ashamed and embarrassed and this puts more stress on him, which tends to continue the behaviour. You need to break this cycle. The key here is to find a balance between using a firm tone of voice when he makes a mistake, and language that encourages him to move forward, at the same time letting him know where he needs to go. Your language needs to be positive and encouraging while conveying your expectation. Remember, he is going to seek your approval and guidance.

To help him break the habit of waiting for the nappy, before bed time I suggest you give him a nice warm bath to relax his muscles and keep him up slightly later; keep underwear on him and his potty out so that he can use it with your guidance. You obviously know what time he has regularly been going so be mindful of this. When he does use the potty, make sure you praise his actions – reinforcing his abilities and giving him your full positive attention, which he is seeking. Perseverance is the key word here; keep calm and carry on. You will get there.

Wiping on His Own

Q *My four-year-old goes to the bathroom independently at nursery, but is expected to clean himself. A combination of rough toilet paper and poor technique are leaving his bottom dirty and his skin irritated. We've tried showing him how to wipe himself and even his baby brother; we practise at home frequently. He still comes home from school dirty. When are most toddlers ready to wipe on their own? How can we teach him to clean his bottom when he's away from home?*

A Your son is obviously making his best efforts to clean his bottom, and as they say, practice will truly make perfect. Four is when most toddlers learn to wipe on their own. Here is something you can teach him at home that will make it easier for him to clean himself, no matter where he is. After he has done his number 2, have him stand up from the toilet and slightly bend his knees, poking his bottom out. He should almost look like a little duckling. This will make the area more accessible for a thorough wiping. The idea is to keep wiping and throwing away paper until it is clean.

You will know when he is getting better as he will have less show on his pants after school. In the meantime what I would do would be to put a little bit of nappy rash cream on his bottom in the morning and when he comes home from school to keep the area from getting more irritated. Also teach him to pull his sleeves up and to tuck his top underneath his chin, so when he wipes his bottom it doesn't touch any of his clothes.

Potty in Public

Q *I'm currently potty-training my two-and-a-half-year-old, and she seems quite confident taking herself off to the potty when she needs to go at home. The problem is when we are out — she refuses to go into public toilets. I always take her favourite potty out with us and constantly reassure her there is nothing to be afraid of, but every time she will start screaming and crying at the very mention of going to the toilet. I have managed to get her to sit on the potty in the corner of the room when we go out to play groups, but this is not convenient to do when we go into a restaurant. At the moment I am taking her back to the car to sit on the potty. I used to have a problem with changing her nappy in the changing rooms so I ended up just going out for short trips so I could avoid taking her into the toilet. We think it's the loud noise of hand dryers that is scaring her, but I can't even get her to go near the toilets to reassure her there is nothing to be frightened of. I'm at my wits' end.*

A The operative word in your question is 'afraid'. Your daughter is frightened. She needs the same privacy in a public place as she has at home. First, at home I would like her to get used to using a training seat on the toilet, rather than a stand-alone potty. Once she gets the hang of that, you can try her out with the training seat in public. To make it less frightening, I would like you first to take her into a public toilet that is designed for one person at a time so that she is not confronted by strangers in the public toilets and so there will be no noise from dryers. Don't worry if, for the first few times, she does nothing when you place her on a public toilet seat with her training seat. What it will do is show her that she is safe enough to relax those muscles to go to the toilet. Once she feels safe, she will get past the fear and you will then be able to graduate to toilets with more than one cubicle. For whatever reason, changing her nappy in the changing rooms created an insecure place for her, so that is what she needs to feel less of now.

Playing with Wee or Poo

Q *My two-year-old daughter drives me insane. When she goes to the toilet, she insists on watching what her wee is doing so it is spraying everywhere. What can I do?*

A It's an innocent thing when children are interested in or play with their wee or poo. Poo is soft and squishy, like putty. Wee is a lot like water, which most kids love to play with. However, this isn't acceptable, as waste is dirty and unhygienic. Your daughter is not deliberately being rebellious towards you or trying to make a mess, she's just discovering where this fascinating water comes from! Use positive non-emotional language to break the habit straight away: 'We don't want wee to go all over the floor. Finish up and we can go and play with some water in the sink.' A similar casual approach is needed if she wants to touch her poo: 'We don't do that, that's dirty, let's flush it away.' Make sure that when the business of number 1 and 2 is done there is the bathroom ritual of flushing and washing hands so she learns hygiene at the same time.

Eating Poo

Q *My two-and-a-half-year-old keeps eating his own poo from his nappy. I have a 16-week-old as well, but he has been doing this since before the baby was born, so I don't think it's to get more attention and I do spend at least two hours twice a week alone with him at a toddler group.*

A Your question, believe it or not, is a very familiar one. Toddlers do all sorts of things in their explorations of the world. My question back to you is: how has your son been left alone long enough to eat his own poo? By now you should have a rough idea of when your child goes poo during the day and how many times. And if you don't, that's the first thing you need to start mentally keeping track of. If he's doing it during nap time, keep checking on him and perhaps he's waking up earlier and trying to 'hide the evidence' of pooing. Eliminate his opportunities to do it. Faeces contain bacteria.

Not Trained at Night

Q *My four-year-old has been completely dry during the day now for just over a year. However, I am still struggling with the night time. I have tried a nightlight, leaving the room lights on and hallway lights . . . nothing seems to motivate him to go. Is this a medical condition or is he just lazy?*

A Let's start off with the positive note. It's great that you have your child potty-trained during the day, so now you need to work out the night time. The age for being completely dry during the night time varies between three and a half and five years old. This depends on a few factors. These are the signs I would like you to look out for:

- Great consistency of regular unprompted bathroom behaviour.

- Bowel movements consistent during the day show discipline to take oneself to the bathroom even in the event of other activities happening.

- He wakes up with a dry nappy several nights in a row.

- You will need to regulate his fluid intake from tea time onwards. It is much harder for the body to hold large amounts of fluid without the need to relieve. If he has a nappy on, he could naturally be relieving himself once in a deep sleep pattern. It's a matter of him becoming more mindful of the urge to go and then prompting himself to act upon it. Perhaps you could leave a potty in his room as he may be apprehensive to get up out of bed and go into the bathroom unaided. Please see my Night-'ish' technique (see box below). This will eventually lead to him getting up himself when he feels the need. But you will need patience and persistence to get to this point. Please get going so you can help him.

THE NIGHT-'ISH' TECHNIQUE

- Around ten or eleven at night, get him up and take him to the bathroom.
- Wake him up enough so he's conscious and aware of what's happening.
- Don't carry him; he should be moving by himself.
- Escort him to the bathroom and let him pull his pants down and go.
- Wash his hands.
- Escort him back to bed.

10

Siblings

The relationship between siblings – whether they're biological or non-biological – is an incredibly special one within the family dynamic. I know from being a sibling myself and being close to my brother what an important relationship it is. As parents you want to be able to nurture that relationship, to do whatever you can to help it be a loving, healthy one. We want that closeness not only in their relationships as children, but also as they grow into adults. The beauty of siblings, whether it's two, three, four or five – is that it can create a *unity* and an ability to support and take care of one another.

Sibling relationships are important not just for the bonds between your children, but also because, in a very real way, they are the foundation of their relationships with the outside world. Ultimately people need to learn how to get along well with other people, whether that's a team of ten in an office or people in our neighbourhood. Sharing, taking turns, compromising, engaging others and being social – toddlers are learning the beginnings of interacting well with others, and when they have siblings, that's who they learn with. Despite being in the same family, they are not born knowing how to get along. So that's why, as much as they may love and enjoy one another, they can drive each other nuts as well at the same time.

Parents often ask me, 'Oh, why do they always bicker?' It's all part of them learning how to be under one roof with their different souls, spirits, personalities and temperaments and forming their own relationships with each other. That's why it's important that you teach them how to interact nicely — they don't just know how to do it on their own. But you also have to know when to referee and when not to. You have to know when to allow them to work things out themselves and not be in the middle of it all the time.

In this section, I address the questions parents commonly ask about helping siblings develop healthy relationships with one another. Whether you have twins, triplets or siblings close together, it can be a handful, especially when they are squabbling among themselves. Sleeping in the same room, not sharing, hurting one another, regression due to a new sibling, juggling the needs of an infant and a toddler . . . this section's got it covered.

IN THIS CHAPTER

- ◆ **Sleeping in the same room**
- ◆ **Coping with multiples**
- ◆ **Fights over toys and food**
- ◆ **Pulling hair**
- ◆ **Constant squabbling**
- ◆ **Playroom chaos**
- ◆ **Copying older siblings**
- ◆ **Jealousy over new baby**
- ◆ **Regression over new baby**
- ◆ **Juggling infant and toddler**

Sleeping in the Same Room

Q *How do you handle a toddler sharing a bedroom with a baby? The baby wakes the toddler, which spirals into a whole-night event where no one gets enough sleep.*

A You don't say how old your baby is. If he is under one, I wouldn't have him share a bedroom with his brother, but keep him in your bedroom. That's because a toddler can crawl into the cot and accidentally smother a baby because he's small. Having the baby with you will also prevent your toddler from being woken during the night. Until a baby is having all of its regular feeds, milk and puree, he is going to experience some sleep disturbances.

Once your younger child is old enough to sleep with his brother, I would suggest settling him to sleep 20 to 30 minutes before your older one's bed time so that he will be soundly asleep before big brother comes in. As for your older child, once his sibling is sleeping in his room, make sure there is an established bed-time routine to settle him into the day-to-night transition. You may want to practise doing this in the afternoon first, so that your toddler understands that people need to be quiet before going to sleep. Read him his story on your bed or in the living room so that when he goes into the bedroom, he understands it's lights out, no talking because his younger brother is asleep.

Coping with Multiples

Q *My husband and I did IVF and now are the parents of triplets. We absolutely love our three-year-old boys, but I'm having trouble keeping it all together, especially as they are now running all over. At the age of 42, this stay-at-home mum can use all the help she can get!*

A Whether you have multiples or kids who are close together in age, parents with several small children need one thing above all: a solid daily routine. A routine helps you better manage your time so you can juggle everyone's needs, including your own. You'll be better organised, which leads to consistency with the triplets in sleeping, eating and playing, which is something all toddlers need.

They'll be well fed and rested and therefore less prone to meltdowns. To establish a routine, start with the fundamentals that are necessary and go from there:

- **Toddlers need at least 10–11 hours or more of sleep each night. What time do they wake up? If it's 6.30 a.m., they need to be in bed at 7.30 p.m.**

- **Once you've got bed time and waking time, you can schedule everything else: breakfast, getting dressed, morning play, lunch, nap, play, dinner, bed-time routine.**

- **Make sure you give yourself more time than you think you'll need so you don't feel rushed. With more than one to deal with, everything takes longer.**

- **When it comes to errands, look at the whole week and pace yourself. You can't keep three three-year-olds out and about all day without problems.**

- **Once you're created the routine, it is all about applying the routine.**

With triplets (or twins and children very close in age), you soon realise it is just inefficient to stagger their care; it becomes much more easy for you to dress, feed, bathe, etc. them all at once. One of the ways parents of multiples get in trouble is trying to deal with one child at a time. Meaning that when parents are pregnant with multiples they have this grand illusion that they will pander to each child individually and the reality of this, when they are born, becomes incredibly taxing on them. All babies need to be taken care of and nurtured properly. So it becomes much more efficient to do the parentcraft needed at the same time. Doing this will allow you enough time to schedule activities to stimulate them on every level and also give you time to enjoy the experience of bonding with each child. Encourage your three-year-olds to become a little more independent so they are doing more and more for themselves, with you as their cheerleader. Be sure to praise them when they achieve their goal and be descriptive with your praise: 'Great, you got your pants on. Now where's your shirt? Can you put that on?'

    Let the non-essentials go! Cleanliness is important but your living room doesn't need to look like the Victoria and Albert Museum. And finally, don't be afraid to ask for help. Contact a multiple support group. Make sure you have some 'me' time each week – perhaps you can hire a mother's helper or ask a relative to give you a break. Parenting multiples is a wonderful experience and a unique one at that – but I realise it can be exhausting, no matter what your age!

Toy Problems

Q *How do I stop my five-year-old interfering with everything my two-and-a-half-year-old is playing with as the toys used to be hers?*

A I've heard this one a thousand times. The reality is that your five-year-old played with those toys, so she remembers and sometimes goes back to them, even though she's too old for them, because there's a sentimental attachment. You need to help her let go. What's really important here is that you don't say, 'They're not yours.' Instead say, 'They used to be yours. They used to belong to you and now we have given them to your brother because you're too old for them and you have new toys that your brother can't play with because he's not old enough yet.' Then lead her to her toys. You can also encourage her to show her brother how to play with the toys and get satisfaction from them that way. As she matures, she'll let go of them.

Pulling Sister's Hair

Q *I'm a mum of 18-month-old twins. My son has a habit of pulling his sister's hair for no reason, which hurts, I know, because she screams at the top of her lungs. He knows what he is doing because he looks right at me, waiting for a response. I've tried talking to him, putting him in the pack and play for a little time out, and having him hug her when he is done with time out. But it still goes on.*

A Whether you have twins or siblings close in age, this bickering behaviour is very common. Here's what your son does know: when he pulls his sister's hair, he gets a reaction from you and from his sister. Firstly, he is too young to be put in a time out. Secondly, he should never be put in a pack and play to show he has done something wrong because they are used for fun and play. What is important is that he learns from your firm voice that what he has just done is not approved. In addition, encourage your twins to give lots of love to one another – hugs, kisses and cuddles.

What you commonly see with this age group is one twin slightly more domineering than the other and a power play starts to take shape as their personalities begin to form. You would have noticed this even when they were babies. One will cry because he needs feeding and the other one will wake up and cry because she now wants what the other has got. If your twins are sharing a train track set or building blocks, they will act no differently than any other children their age. One child will always recognise that he can get what he wants by being more dominant. So encouraging your twins to do things both separately and together is most important here so they learn to get along but also have their own autonomy. Let them do puzzles together but separately. Let them finger-paint one large piece of paper together and separately, have them share one play chest together but dress separately. Singing nursery rhymes where they act, move and sing together, playing together.

Constant Sibling Warfare

Q *My three daughters (two, three and five) are constantly bickering over their toys and games. I feel like I spend all my time refereeing their squabbles and I'm sick of it. I want to tell them to work it out on their own, but I know that a two-year-old can't stand up to a sister who's five.*

A Three girls squabbling every 15 minutes can certainly be an ear sore and I'm sure there are some days that are easier than others. The truth is your two-, three- and five-year-olds cannot work it out for themselves. I do believe it is a matter of what they are bickering over. Have they learnt to share the toys that belong to them all? Are some of the toys that belong to them individually being picked up to play with without permission? Do two of the three play together, making one feel left out? Or is the older one getting frustrated because the other two won't obey her direction? All of these examples are healthy developmental stages of your daughters' bonding and social skills. Of course there will be a large number of 'it's not fair's thrown in there and that's why you have to get to the bottom of the 'who started it' drama. Here are the facts: your two-year-old is learning right from wrong, your three-year-old has just started to remember it, and your five-year-old knows it and is testing it. My suggestions:

♦ **Set clear expectations of behaviour.**

♦ **Any behaviour that breaks the rules, like hurting another person, will lead to the Sideline or Naughty Step technique if it does not stop after a warning is given.**

♦ **Take time to observe their behaviour. Observation allows you to take note of exactly what is going on so you can correctly resolve the situation.**

Playroom Chaos

Q *I have five-year-old triplets, who are fortunate enough to have their own playroom. All my boys are extremely spoilt by our extended family members. Walking into their playroom is like walking into Hamley's. You would think that they would be in toy paradise, but they do nothing but argue with one another, fight and sometimes, when they get angry, break each other's toys. I am at my wits' end and I feel like bagging up all their toys and leaving them with one as a lesson. What can you suggest?*

A Who says 'Toys keep them quiet?' They need to learn how to respect their own toys, let alone those of their siblings'. So look at the technique below and I suggest you implement it ASAP.

SHARING BIN TECHNIQUE

- Get three large bins or cardboard boxes and put each child's name on one bin.

- Lay out all your children's toys.

- Go through the toys and decide which toy belongs to each person and have him put it away in his bin.

- After all the toys have been put somewhere, ask each of them to choose one toy from his bin that he will share with his brothers.

- When they've successfully shared these toys among themselves for the week, give them another bin and label it Sharing Bin. Ask them each to pick a few toys that can go into the Sharing Bin and explain that these belong to all of them. Change the toys in the Sharing Bin every few months.

Q *I have three toddlers and they all want different kinds of food at meal times. At least one of them starts to cry if they don't get what they want and I do feel out of control. Once I've served up their food onto plates, they argue about the plates I've given them and my daughter sometimes throws her food on the floor because she wants her brother's plate! What do I do to make them get along? Tea times are terrible.*

A This is not about running Jo's Café here. I mean, seriously. Why are you serving different meals? To offer different choices and cook three meals allows them to argue about wanting what the other is having. That's just a recipe for disaster, excuse the pun! It's natural behaviour for toddlers to keep changing their minds because they want what the other ones are having and don't want to feel as if they're missing out. They want to be treated *fairly* and *equally*. And the only way you can treat them fairly and equally is to give them all the same food.

Tea times are terrible because you're not being assertive enough in the situation. Don't give them a reason to argue. Cook one meal unless one is allergic to it. If you want to give them choices, do it at snack time so if they change their minds it doesn't matter – raisin box or fruit tube, it's easy to switch.

I would also suggest that you give each their own special plastic plate and cup, whether that's Dora the Explorer for one, Toy Story for the next, etc. Or, if you want to help them learn to take turns, rotate who gets to choose which plate first, second and third. But *you* have to be the person who decides the order: 'It's you who's going first today, you who's going second and you who's going third.' And when someone says, 'Why did he get to go first?' 'He took the one I wanted!' you say, 'Why did he go first? Because I made that choice and tomorrow you'll be first.' Parents need to realise that they can't please all their children at the same time! There's always someone who's a bit disappointed. But there's a serious, beautiful lesson in that – we all have to take turns. That's the way life is.

Copying Older Siblings

Q *My three-year-old toddler is constantly copying what his older siblings are doing — climbing, hitting, screaming. I am at the end of my tether.*

A No wonder you are at the end of your rope. Your home life sounds like it's not very peaceful. Yes your toddler is imitating his siblings, but why are his older brothers and sisters so out of control? That to me seems like the bigger problem. You are going to need a big dose of consistency, persistence and patience to turn your household around. You need a written set of house rules that you make clear to them all. Then when they break the rules, put the Naughty Step in place (see pages 26–27) or time out in their rooms if the older ones are too old for the Naughty Step (past age seven or so). Since you have let them become so out of control, you are going to have to be really consistent and follow through every single time so they all get the point that you really mean it now.

While you are instituting some discipline and control, at the same time you must also create positive experiences for and with all your children. Are they getting enough mental and physical stimulation? Do they have a chance to run around outside for an hour a day? Do they have challenging games and toys to play with? They may be fighting with one another because they are bored and don't have enough physical outlet.

As well as discipline, give them opportunities to please you — give them age-appropriate chores to do — and praise them for doing the tasks well. Give the older ones more responsibility and privileges. Praise also when they play nicely together and are kind to one another. Find ways to do things together as a family that are positive, like going to a pool, a camping ground or an amusement park. The balance between teaching them proper behaviour and having more fun should turn things around for you all.

Jealousy over the New Baby

Q *My 20-month-old is jealous over her new baby brother's arrival. I am constantly telling her 'no' when it comes to her new brother because she is not gentle. She hits him, pokes him in the eye and squeezes* *his nose so he can't breathe. I want her to interact with him, but I don't want her to hurt him. I certainly never leave them in a room alone together. How can I make her be kind and enjoy her brother?*

A Yes, you absolutely cannot leave your baby alone with your toddler. Your daughter has recognised that she'll get more of your time if she behaves badly towards her younger brother. By hurting him, she not only gets your attention but she also gets to express her jealousy over this transition in the only way she knows how. She feels a little bit threatened by all the attention, time and comfort the baby is receiving. That's natural.

Understand that it's not the baby she doesn't like, it's the position she's been put in. The good news is that this is typically a short phase, it really is. Don't over-react. When does she hurt her brother the most? When she's around Dad or Mum? That's who she is more likely to get a reaction from. This is not a case of doing the Naughty Step. She is far too young for that anyway. This is more about understanding the emotional meltdown with this new transition. When she does try to hurt him, instead of you being cross with her, she needs to see disappointment from you: 'No, that's not how we treat him.' Then remove her from the baby. Tell her she can come up on the sofa and participate with you and the baby if she behaves. Reward her with praise when she's kind.

You can also buy her a doll 'from the baby' so she can play pretend. When you bathe the baby, she can bathe her dolly. This can help her feel included.

Make sure she has time with just you. There's a difference between one-on-one time with the baby present and one-on-one without the baby. Your daughter knows if she completely has you to herself or not. Find a balance with both and have times when you leave the house with your daughter and really do things one-on-one.

It's also very important that you spend time with the two of them together because she has to get used to having the baby around. The positive way to get round this is to make her the big girl: 'Isn't the baby lucky to have a big sister like you?' Your language is also important. Don't say, 'We can't go out now because the baby needs to eat.' That makes it seem as if it's all about the baby and that her needs and wants don't matter. Instead, say, 'Yes, we can go out, but I'm just going to feed the baby first and then we'll go.'

Toddler Regressing after Baby Arrives

Q *My three-year-old son suddenly regressed when his baby sister arrived. He wants to be carried everywhere and suddenly refuses to feed himself. It feels like I've got two infants. What can I do to get my toddler back?*

A Regression is very common when a new sibling arrives. It happens because a toddler unconsciously thinks that their position as the 'baby' has been taken away and that Mummy and Daddy love the baby and so I need to be a baby so they will love me. It can show up in any number of ways – refusing to dress himself, regressing in potty-training, eating or walking, acting up, even wanting to nurse again. If you deal appropriately with it, regression typically lasts not more than a month.

So how should you handle it? As calmly and matter-of-factly as possible. If you get angry or impatient, your toddler learns that he can get a reaction from you and then it may become a power struggle that goes on much longer.

THE BIG SIB TECHNIQUE

The trick here is to help him believe that being the big sibling is the best thing to be.

♦ **Think in terms of responsibilities and privileges: 'You can go with Daddy to music because you're a big boy, the baby can't.' 'You can walk all by yourself so we can go to the train, the baby can't.' 'You can put your shoes on by yourself because you're a big boy, the baby can't.'**

♦ **Make him a Big Brother sticker that he gets when he does what it is you want him to – walk by himself, dress himself, etc.**

Meet him halfway. If he won't feed himself, have him do one spoonful and then you do one. Make him go first. Then have him do two and you do one. Then three to your one. He puts on his shirt and you put on his trousers. As for carrying, make sure you have plenty of cuddle and hug times, but when you need him to walk, calmly remind him he's a big boy and can walk himself. Use the Big Sib technique to get him excited about being the older one.

Juggling Infant and Toddler

Q *I'm finding it difficult to follow through with the Naughty Step for my two-and-a-half-year-old when my ten-month-old needs my attention. How do I continue to put my toddler on the Step if my baby is crying and needs me?*

A I know it's hard to balance two but it's likely that your older one is taking advantage of that to act up just when the baby cries. So you can't let her misbehaviour slide. It's a juggling act – sometimes you may be able to pick up the baby and deal with your older one. Another time you might need to leave the baby crying a bit longer. One thing you can do when the older one is acting up is say to her, 'This is not okay. I will be right back to deal with it.' Try to come back ASAP as toddlers don't have long attention spans. And whatever else you do, make sure you keep the baby out of the line of fire if you have a toddler who throws or hits when she gets angry. You must keep your infant safe.

11

Sleep

Getting to sleep, staying in bed, staying asleep all night . . . Whatever the situation at your house, sleep deprivation can sometimes feel like an art that toddlers have mastered! And yet it is crucially important that toddlers – and parents – get enough sleep. Proper sleep is associated with ability to focus and concentrate, positive mood, memory, even the ability to maintain a healthy weight. You can't be at your best as a parent and your children can't be at their best to grow and learn if you don't all get enough sleep.

As a parent, it keeps you with a longer fuse. You have more tolerance and patience, experience less stress. You have the endurance and perseverance to follow things through. You don't feel foggy. You have more clarity so you make good decisions. You enjoy your days with your children more. When your toddler gets enough sleep, she's less irritable and more upbeat too. She has more patience to learn new things and the ability to concentrate that learning requires. Her ability to remember what she's learning is at its best. She has greater resilience when faced with challenges, too, so she isn't as likely to melt down over the smallest things.

The National Sleep Foundation recommends that toddlers between the ages of one and three get 12 to 14 hours of sleep in a 24-hour period. For three-to-five-year-olds, the recommendation is 11 to 13 hours. And for us adults it's seven to nine hours.

Are you and your toddler getting enough sleep? If not, what is standing in the way? Toddlers often resist going to bed and staying there. Do you have trouble getting her into bed at a decent time? Or staying there once the bed-time routine is done? Does she wake up in the night and end up in your room? Or do you have a too-early riser on your hands? Are nap times a struggle? Did you have a good routine going and then it got disrupted? Whatever the issue that's keeping you and your little ones from getting enough sleep, I hope you now understand why it is crucially important that you resolve it. I know that if you follow my suggestions and techniques in this chapter, you can soon be experiencing a good night's sleep for all. Good Night . . . ZZZZZZZZZZZZZZZZ

IN THIS CHAPTER

- ◆ **Waking at night**
- ◆ **Move to bed from cot**
- ◆ **Fighting nap time**
- ◆ **Early hours waking**
- ◆ **Mum losing temper over sleep issues**
- ◆ **Staying in bed**
- ◆ **Move to new bedroom**
- ◆ **Getting kids into own bed**
- ◆ **Serious sleep problem versus bad habit**

Waking at Night

Q *My daughter is 16 months old and the last couple of weeks she has started waking in the night. When I go into her room and do what I have always done, which is rub her back and stroke her head to help get her back off to sleep, she just goes crazy in her cot – kicking, pushing my hand away, becoming hysterical! When my partner goes into the room she calms down immediately. I can only assume she wants him because she hardly sees him as he doesn't get home till right before her bed time. If I am honest it's killing me inside as I feel like I don't have that bond with her at night that a mum should have. In the day she is fine with me and I can settle her. We have been using the technique where you go in and reassure every five minutes. We were thinking we should both go into her room at night for a while.*

A It's always hard for a parent when a child favours one over the other for pacifying. It could very well be because she misses him. Try not to take it personally. You spend all day with her and have wonderful moments where you are able to bond and have fun. I wouldn't feel the need to have to do it all. Children switch around their preferences all the time. One minute it is Mummy they want cuddles from, the next minute it is Daddy. You state in your question you have used a technique where you go in every five minutes. It obviously has not been reassuring her and I personally feel she is at an age where she needs to learn how to self-soothe. I would like to recommend my Controlled Timed Crying technique, alternating the nights as to who goes in (see box on page 182).

Don't despair. Trust the technique and turn this around. After using the Controlled Timed Crying technique, another previously dismayed parent in a similar situation emailed me later to say: 'All is well and quiet at our house . . . my child finally gets the point that 'I'M NOT PICKING YOU UP, GO TO SLEEP'. Lots of time to love her later.'

THE CONTROLLED TIMED CRYING TECHNIQUE

Practise this during nap times too. You're teaching your toddler how to soothe herself to sleep without you. It may take up to a week to work and you must be consistent.

- **Kiss your toddler and then place them in the cot, say night night, and walk out.**
- **The first time she cries, go in, put her hand on her tummy and say 'shhh', just once in a comforting tone, then leave the room.**
- **Wait five minutes and if she's still crying, repeat the routine.**
- **If she still cries, go back in 10 minutes and then, if necessary, in 20.**
- **Continue to do the technique, doubling the time as necessary: 10, 20, 40, 80 minutes.**
- **Resist picking her up or she'll think she's getting out of bed and when you put her back in the cot she will scream even more than before.**
- **Refrain from talking to her. The only noise you should be making is the comforting noise of 'shhhhhhh'. This allows the child to recognise that it is night time. A time when we rest and sleep and do not talk.**

Up Every 20 Minutes

Q *My 15-month-old son sleeps for twenty minutes at a time on a good night. He is constantly on the move and has plenty of stimulation through the day, he is in a routine with everything else – meals, bath time, going down to sleep on his own is no problem. It's just staying asleep. I'm at my wits' end, which doesn't help I know!*

A Sporadic sleep of 20 minutes is no fun for anyone and doesn't allow your son to get the amount of uninterrupted sleep that he needs. It is common, around 12 and 15 months, to see kids wake up during the night to test the boundaries of rules and the schedule you have set for them. It's a stage when kids get rather clingy and some even have separation anxiety. It's also a prime time for colds, teething, growth spurts and a change in behaviour. It will be important that when he does wake up, he is not pacified with a dummy or another bottle or a beaker. All this pandering with different aids to pacify him will teach him he can get up and receive more. Please make sure that:

- **Your child is sleeping at least two hours during the day in a consistent daytime routine, otherwise he can become over-tired.**

- **He has a decent bed time. I would suggest waking up no later than 3 p.m. from nap time and going to bed at 7 p.m.**

- **He is stimulated enough physically and mentally during his waking hours, otherwise he's not getting challenged; instead of getting tired he is bored.**

- He's eating appropriate and healthy proportions so he doesn't go to bed hungry.

- He has a bed-time routine that allows you to spend enough time to create a wind-down period.

- His nappy is dry, he and the room are warm.

- You use the Controlled Timed Crying technique (see page 182) if needed.

Hang in there, because you will come out of the place you're in now. Please note that it will be important for you to observe how your son is during the day, as sporadic waking intervals can also be a sign of teething or poorliness, especially if it is unusual behaviour for him.

Move to Bed

Q *At what age do you generally move toddlers from a cot to a bed? I know it seems like a stupid question, but I really have no idea.*

A I see no rush to move a child from a cot to a bed unless she's grown out of it and the cot has become too narrow a space to sleep in. If she's sleeping well, it's definitely not worth disrupting her. As you can see from the next question, moving from cot to bed can be a big change for a toddler and can create temporary sleep problems.

Transition to Bed

Q *We have a little boy who is almost two. We have just changed his cot to a toddler bed and although he was sleeping really well all through the night and going to sleep by himself, he now just screams unless one of us is in the room. He is also waking in the night, which is a killer, as I often only get back from work at 11.30 p.m.*

Your son is experiencing the adjustment from cot to bed. I generally don't advise making the switch until he's actually outgrown the cot. But you've already done it, so hang in there, he'll adjust. To deal with his screaming unless you are in the room, you should try the Sleep Separation technique (see box below) because it helps with the separation anxiety that two-year-olds go through. Make sure that you put what was in your son's cot in his bed too. Maybe he had two favourite cuddly toys and a familiar blankie. If you have bought him a single bed make sure that he is safe, so that he doesn't fall out easily. Get him playing in his room during the day so that he can get used to this big-sized cot he can now call his bed.

THE SLEEP SEPARATION TECHNIQUE

- ◆ Complete your usual night-time routine. After your cuddle, say good night, and tell him it's time to close his eyes and go to sleep.

- ◆ Turn the lights off, leave the door ajar and sit adjacent to his bed or cot out of arm's reach. Do not get into bed with him.

- ◆ Stay sitting in silence until he goes to sleep. If he tries to talk, don't answer him, and if he gets out of bed just place him gently back into bed. If he tries to run out of the room you will have to close the bedroom door, so make sure you have a low nightlight in the room.

- ◆ Repeat the same steps the next night, but this time sit a little further away until eventually you are sitting outside the door with the door open and then don't have to do it at all.

Fighting Nap Time

Q   *My daughter is 15 months old and she has been transitioned from a single morning nap to an after-lunch nap. This has worked great when she's at the child-minder's. But for me at home she won't sleep. She either goes into the crib and hangs out, talking, giggling and having a ball throwing her dummy out of the cot, or she cries on and off until I can't take it. Is it okay that she just hangs out in the cot or should I try to get her to sleep with rocking and cuddles? I need her to take a nap – I need my alone time to do things around the house.*

A   At her age, your daughter should be sleeping consistently in the afternoons for one to two hours, not just resting. If she's hanging out in the cot talking and giggling, then she might not be tired yet and that means you're putting her down too early after lunch. In the mornings before nap time, do things with your daughter that will stimulate her mentally, like number- and shape-sorting, flash cards, making the sounds with animals, floor puzzles – things that will again mentally stimulate her and also make her get physically tired so that by the time she has lunch, she'll feel sleepy. If she eats at noon, she may not be ready to sleep till 1 or 1.30. If it works for the minder, then trust me, it will work for you. Talk to her and see what type of things she does. Remember your child-minder has a structure in place and you will need to create the same for your little one so that she benefits. That will then in return give you some time to do as you please.

Once nap time is upon you, create a ritual for napping by closing the curtains in her room and putting her under her covers. Then stay out. If she's throwing her dummy out of the cot and crying and you are going into her room and putting the dummy back in her cot, then you have a nice little game going on! Why would she go to sleep when there's a fun game to play? And what does 'I can't take it' mean? Does that mean you go in and pick her up? Because if it does, then she knows just how to get out of that cot. No picking up, rocking or cuddles. If you need to, use the Controlled Timed Crying technique on page 182.

Early Hours Waking

Q *Our little girl turned three years old last month; since that time we have had lots of trouble with early morning waking. She wakes at 4.30 a.m. and screams to go to the toilet. She gets taken to the toilet and returns to bed but then kicks her door, screaming until one of us gives in and gets up. We also have a seven-month-old daughter who wakes at the same time, but with the dummy replaced in her mouth she's happy to sleep until 6.30-ish. Friends have suggested putting a TV in our three-year-old's room so she can watch a DVD to keep quiet, but we are reluctant to do this. Should we put her to bed later? She throws tantrums if she stays up past 7.30 p.m.*

A Very clearly, your three-year-old has taken it upon herself to use her seven-month-old sister as ransom to get her own way. Clearly, when she screams and kicks you will give in to her antics for fear of waking up your youngest. As soon as she screams, it will be important for you to go into her room, and without raising your voice, speak to her in an authoritative tone that indicates disapproval of her behaviour. Let her know that it is still night time and everybody still needs to go to sleep. Tell her that you expect her to go back to sleep and in the morning, when she wakes up, if she wants to play in her bedroom she can. Let her know that if she chooses to misbehave she will miss out on a privilege the next day. I have suggested to some parents that they buy an alarm clock. When the animal farm alarm sound goes off, it is an indication that it is morning and time to get up. I agree with you that I would not start putting a television in her room. This becomes an awful habit and one that many rely on and sometimes become very complacent with. It becomes a hard habit to break once you have started.

Mum Losing Her Temper over Sleep Issues

Q *I have a 21-month-old daughter. She was a perfect sleeper since she was a baby. The problem started when I let her sleep on the settee on her afternoon nap one day last month. Now she refuses to go to her cot and she will only fall asleep on the settee. We then carry her to her cot. If she wakes up in the night she screams the place down until she is allowed*

*to sleep on the settee. Even worse, she refuses to go to sleep although very
tired and stays up until 11.30 p.m. I tried the Controlled Timed Crying
technique, which turned into uncontrolled crying by me. She looked terrified,
holding her breath and having hiccups from crying. I am trying to exhaust
her, and cut her midday nap, but she is still the same.*

*The other night unfortunately I lost it. I was yelling at her, shaking her,
throwing her like a rag doll on the bed. I'm even ashamed to admit I put
my hand over her mouth to try to muffle her screaming at 4.00 a.m. Then
I cried, feeling like a totally inadequate, hopeless and helpless mother.*

A Thank you for being brave enough to speak out. I know you know you
need to seek help. The situation has quite clearly become overwhelming
for you and has got to the point where you feel completely defeated. IT IS NOT
OKAY EVER TO SHAKE, MUFFLE THE MOUTH OF OR THROW YOUR CHILD.
Your story is a clear example of how easy it is to lose control. If you ever feel
like your patience is being tested, and you are completely overwhelmed and
feel deep desperation inside, leave your child in the cot crying and contact the
24-hour free Parent Support Hotline: http://www.nspcc.org.uk, 0800 1111.
Calls are confidential. Had this action been fatal, you would have been calling
an ambulance.

SO LOOK. Here is where we are at. I want you to take a deep breath and
know clearly that what has happened here is that you have set up a bad habit that
we now need to break. Time to go back to the healthy pattern:

* **You need to re-establish the bed-time routine. I would suggest bath
time, pyjamas and stories in her bedroom, and then off to bed.**

* **She obviously became accustomed to spending time with you both on
the sofa, afraid of missing out on anything. So you will have to establish
the daytime nap in the same fashion as the night-time. No resting on
the sofa, but resting in her cot. Place a few books and cuddlies in her
cot and tell her it is rest time.**

* **I would suggest that you and your partner together do the Controlled
Timed Crying technique on page 182 to re-establish her sleeping
pattern.**

♦ Last but not least, I think that it is very important that you talk with your local GP about what has just happened, or speak to a health visitor at a local clinic. Because you could be over-anxious, hormonally unbalanced and/or suffering from post-natal depression. It's very important for you to identify how you are feeling right now. With medical help one can identify the situation and get immediate help for it. Millions of women around the world feel at their wits' end. The fact that you got to the point of acting out your thoughts shows me that it would clearly benefit the whole family to get help.

Staying in Bed

Q I have a three-year-old son who has been climbing out of his cot for several weeks now and only wants to sleep in our guest bedroom. So we figured it was time to replace his cot and got a toddler bed for his room. The first night he slept, no problem. The second and third nights he came out about 50 times each. We used positive reinforcement for the first 15 times, and after that we threatened taking away toys. Finally, we took all the toys out of his room and he eventually fell asleep.

The next morning, I decided to try and make a chart for the days of the week and each morning if he stayed in his bed, he'd get a sticker and then we'd do something on the reward list. He stayed in his bed for one night and then we went out for pizza as a reward. But the following night, again he was out until all hours of the evening until I finally said to my husband, let's put him in our bed, and he fell asleep right away.

I am not the type of mummy to have kids stay in my bed; I am not a softy at all! We're trying everything, we stopped napping him so he'd be tired for bed time, but that is turning out to be a disaster because he is a wreck by 2 p.m. I even put on some lullaby music and that put him to sleep the next night, but failed to work last night. We're all exhausted and need sleep!

A When I read this, it makes me feel dizzy. One minute he was in the guest bedroom, then he was in a toddler bed, then in your bed, then he was going out for pizza and then he was up all night. Now, you're giving him a concert with music and he's wondering what you're going to give him next time!

The problem is there's no consistency. You keep trying different things without giving any one of them a chance to work. Pick something and make up your mind that you're not giving in, one way or the other. I would put a bedrail on the side of his bed so he doesn't fall out of it. I would create a proper bed-time routine for him so that he doesn't feel like he's being rushed to bed. I would read stories, come out of the room, and use the Stay in Bed technique (see box below). Stick with it – with consistency no technique takes longer than seven days. It doesn't matter how many times he comes out, you have to be consistent with your response.

I once put a three-year-old who had never been in her own room in bed with the Stay in Bed technique. It took an hour and forty-five minutes the first night. The second night took three attempts. The third night, she went in her bed and stayed there. Your son is going to keep pushing unless you stay consistent. Children like routine and consistency; it makes them feel safe and secure.

THE STAY IN BED TECHNIQUE

- ◆ **When your child gets out of bed, take him back to bed with a simple, 'It's bed time darling.' Ignore all excuses except potty – and that only once.**

- ◆ **The next time he gets up, usher him back with just 'Bed time'.**

- ◆ **By the third time he gets up, put him back without saying a word. Stay calm. Avoid eye contact as your eyes speak volumes and don't communicate in any way at any cost. He'll say, 'Why aren't you talking to me?' Say nothing.**

- ◆ **Repeat again and again if need be; sooner or later he'll give up.**

- ◆ **Use a reward chart to tick off trouble-free nights. When he gets to four, he can have a reward. But something small, you don't want him acting up to get a prize.**

Move to a New Bedroom

Q *We are expecting a baby in five months and have moved our three-year-old to a new room, as the nursery will be for the baby. He has the same bed and bedding, yet his room is not attached to ours any more. It is on another level and is much larger. It's been four nights and it is a fight every night. We have trouble getting him to go to sleep and then he is up anywhere from 3 a.m. to 5 a.m. at our bedside, refusing to go back to his room. We're all very tired. I feel like I have a newborn again, already!*

A Do not despair, you are simply in the middle of his transition to the new room. Just because you have mentally made up your mind that this is where he is going to sleep doesn't mean he is going to settle in the same amount of time.

There are two things at play here. Not only has he moved to a new, larger room not attached to the security of his parents' room, he's also on a whole different level of the house. You have to have realistic expectations of how long this will take – and four nights is unrealistic. The good thing is, you have started this five months before the arrival of the baby, which is fabulous. Here are a few tips for you:

◆ **Put some toys in your son's bedroom and play with him there during the day. Invite a play friend round and let him show off his new bedroom to his play date.**

◆ **Put a baby monitor in his room and tell him this is where Mummy can hear him and that she's not that far away.**

◆ **Give him at least three to four weeks to get comfortable with filling in the 'boots' of this bigger space.**

◆ **Do the Sleep Separation technique with him (see page 185).**

Getting Kids into Beds after Co-Sleeping

Q *I'm a mother who believes in co-sleeping. I breast-fed my two children until they were three. When they were younger, four of us in the bed and the dog wasn't such a big deal. I just can't get them to sleep in their own beds now and I end up on the floor most nights. This has put a strain on my relationship and the dog spends more time sleeping with my husband than I do these days. Help!*

A Yes, help is much needed. I personally don't believe in co-sleeping with infants because of an increased risk of smothering and overheating. But, you obviously made the choice to do so in your family. Now it is time to move your children on in their development. Plus it seems like all of you are

trying unsuccessfully to get enough sleep. And the strain on your relationship doesn't help the situation! I would recommend you to do the Sleep Separation technique (page 185) or the Stay in Bed technique (page 190) so that your children learn to sleep in their own beds. It is as important for them to self-soothe, and be comfortable in their own beds and actually get a good night's sleep, as it is for you and your husband to get a good night's sleep because sleep deprivation ends up disturbing the whole family. It creates poor diet habits, a lack of attention and focus, irritability and a lack of patience and perseverance.

Get your children used to playing in their rooms during the day. It will help them for the night time. And let them take ownership of their rooms by colouring in their names and hanging their art work up so that they become places they enjoy being in.

Once you've made up your mind which technique you're going to do, stick to it. Tag-team with your partner so it's not just you doing it. You've become the human pacifier and now they don't want to be on their own. But they'll get used to it.

Sick of Pushchair for Sleeping

Q *I've been working as a nanny for a family who have two very active boys. The oldest is three and the youngest is 16 months. For the past eight months, in order to get the 16-month-old to sleep, I have been pushing him in a pushchair till he falls asleep. I've tried putting him in his cot and letting him cry it out, but I don't want to let him cry too long. I don't want to take the risk of upsetting my boss. But he's getting too big to push around and rock every day to get him to sleep. I've tried laying him on the couch so he can go to sleep like his big brother, but he just gets up and starts jumping on it. For a week, he'd go to sleep on his own. Then my husband and I went on holiday. When I came back, it was like he'd never fallen asleep on his own. I am at my wits' end and seriously need some advice on how to deal with this in a way that will not upset my employer.*

As a nanny it is your duty to look after the kids and to let the parents know they're upsetting their son's routine. No doubt he's over-tired and he doesn't want to eat, doesn't want to play, and soon it will be upsetting everything else. You're saying you don't want to upset your boss, but at the end of the day, they're rocking him as well. Your job as a nanny is to put the health and welfare of the child first. They will thank you for it. Here are the steps you should follow so you can get the kids back on track and you and your employers on the same page:

- ◆ Sit down and talk to the parents about it, full stop. You should have an open, honest conversation about this little boy being 16 months old and that he should be sleeping in his own bed.

- ◆ That conversation should lead to an agreement as to what technique you are going to use.

- ◆ At 16 months, he should be sleeping twice a day: once in the morning and once in the afternoon.

- ◆ You are going to have to implement the technique in his bedroom. As he's 16 months, he will be going through some separation anxiety. So, what I suggest you do is the Sleep Separation technique (see page 185).

Serious Sleep Problem or Bad Habit?

When are sleep problems a serious problem and not just a bad habit? I am worried there is something wrong with my son. He wakes up at least four times a night, crying and screaming, and I don't know whether he is having nightmares or if there are noises from the street waking him in the night. I'm exhausted and beginning not to be able to cope. It's also putting a strain on my relationship with my husband as he says leave him to cry. We are just all so tired!

To figure out what's going on here, I would recommend you do a mental checklist and ask yourself the following questions:

- **Are there noises that are awakening him?**

- **Is it dark enough in the room?**

- **Has he had enough food so he's not waking up from being hungry?**

- **Has he been mentally and physically stimulated enough so that he's tired and ready to go to sleep in the evening?**

- **How are you responding when he cries? Do you give him milk or food when he wakes up? Do you go in and talk to him? Allow him to come into your bed? The body has a built-in alarm clock and if you are giving him something, whether it is attention or food, he may wake up automatically at that time to get it.**

- **Could it be night terrors? Night terrors are when a child might scream, thrash, kick and/or cry while asleep. The child is not really awake and settles down again after a few minutes. They are not nightmares because there are no images with them. They usually occur about two to three hours after falling asleep. They can be frightening to a parent because they are so dramatic, but children have no memory of them when they wake up because they were in deep sleep when they happened. They are not indications of a medical problem and children eventually grow out of them. Talk to your GP if you are concerned about this.**

Once you've gone through this checklist, hopefully you will see what's going on and have a better idea of what you need to do. If how you're responding is making him wake up, then, yes, you're creating a bad habit which you can address with the Controlled Timed Crying technique (see page 182).

12

Temperament and Personality

As parents learn very quickly, little ones come into the world with their own carved-out personalities and temperaments. Some are more active, others are quieter. Some are bold, others less risk-taking. When you understand your little one's unique personality and temperament, you can work with it rather than struggle against it. You know, for instance, you have to be more diligent about safety with a child with a more risk-taking temperament. So you put even more safeguards in place rather than wait for falls to happen.

That being said, I don't believe in using this awareness and knowledge to put up with misbehaviour. All toddlers need to learn boundaries and rules and be given consequences for not following them. I also don't approve of using temperament and personality differences to put children in pigeon holes – to label him 'the defiant one' or 'the fearful one'. Because I believe that doing so limits your ability as parents to help your children develop to their full potential and it can certainly produce tensions between siblings as they grow up.

However, becoming more aware of your child's temperament and personality helps you to understand how to relate to her and how to encourage her. It may be true that, given who your child is, you have to work harder at making her feel comfortable in new surroundings if she is a child who tends to be more fearful, or have to be even more conscientious with follow-through with discipline if a child is very strong-willed. This section offers advice on these kinds of considerations. It looks at some of the most common temperament and personality issues parents of toddlers ask me about: dealing with wilfulness, shyness, not being able to let things go, melodrama and anger.

IN THIS CHAPTER

◆ **Working with a child's temperament**

◆ **Strong-willed child**

◆ **Letting things go**

◆ **Dramatic personality**

◆ **Shy**

◆ **Angry**

Do I Just Have to Put Up with His Temperament?

Q   *I was wondering whether, because I was a handful as a toddler and my three-year-old is one now, is it just in us to be that way? Or can I change how he screams and throws tantrums?*

A   Scientists have discovered that babies are born with a certain temperament and that temperaments do run in families. So it is true that he probably inherited his wilfulness from you. Hopefully the experience with your son might give you some empathy for your own parents! I think this is the bit where your parents say, 'Now you know how I felt.'

The fact that he's wilful absolutely doesn't mean, however, that you must simply put up with his naughty behaviour. What it does mean is that you have to be absolutely consistent with discipline when he acts up and that you follow my tantrum steps (see pages 90–91) every time he throws a fit. It might take you longer, but you can teach him the proper way to behave. Think of it this way: in the battle of wills between you, you need to make sure you don't stand down and that you mean what you say!

That being said, don't fight unnecessary battles – only the crucial ones. Let him pick out his own clothes, give him food choices within reason, make sure he gets to choose some activities during the day that he wants to do. Offer as much freedom and independence as possible, while insisting on proper behaviour.

Strong-willed Child

Q   *My husband and I are about to go crazy. We have a three-year-old little girl whom we adopted from China when she was 15 months old. She is VERY stubborn, does NOT listen at all, kicks and hits our dog and throws things when she gets angry. We have not been able to find the right discipline for her. We have tried time out, tried telling her, 'When I count to five you'd better have done this or that or you will be in time out' or 'If these toys are not picked by the time I count to five, I will throw them out.' She always fights me to put her clothes on, she usually starts kicking her legs and ends up kicking me. We are STILL trying to get her to sleep in her own room. I don't know what to do any more.*

A As you said at the beginning of your question, you have a child with a temperament of her own, who wants everything on her own terms. This kind of behaviour either happens when a three-year-old hasn't had any consistent rules or boundaries or with a three-year-old who is emotionally very young indeed and finds it hard to adapt to new situations. I really feel the exercise here is to concentrate on her auditory skills so she is able to listen and take more direction. The fact that she hits the dog shows that she is taking out her frustrations on the family pet. That behaviour needs to be curbed with the Naughty Step (see pages 26–27). Some children, when they get angry, throw what is in their hands and this is a matter of coming down to her eye level and, using a very firm voice, telling her what you expect from her.

However, what I fail to see is a mention of anything this little girl does do that lightens your heart. It's all negative! It doesn't seem like a happy home to be in right now because everyone is in a downward spiral. Yes, your little girl needs to learn your word is final on some things, but you also need to set her up for success. What she really wants to do is to please you, and the more she messes up, the more frustrated she gets.

You can turn things around with positive parenting. Encourage her to do things that she is able to achieve. Give her much praise and reward so she will want to continue behaving positively. If you yourselves are very strong characters and all you do is dictate in a hostile tone, then she is naturally going to fight for some control back. Help her develop self-sufficiency, lighten your tone, let her try and put her own clothes on first. Set in place tasks where she can get a sense of achievement and feel proud of herself, like helping with setting the table and taking care of the dog. You create the environment she is in, so make it a positive one because change really does happen quickly when a family sets their mind to it. The good news is that she is only three years old and, at that age, behaviour patterns change really quickly.

Problem with Persistence?

Q *Recently my three-year-old son lost one of his favourite trucks. We looked high and low, but couldn't find it. But he wouldn't let it go. He kept asking for it again and again till I thought I would go mad. Is there such a thing as too much persistence?*

A Toddlers can get stuck on things. It's not an issue to worry about as a lasting personality trait. If you can't find something he's lost, don't make yourself crazy. Keep it light. Tell your child, 'We've looked, it's around here somewhere, it will show up.' Then distract him by getting him engaged in something else. If he keeps asking, don't ignore his requests, but rather show him that you've listened to him and acted upon his concern – 'Remember we looked and couldn't find it?' I would suggest giving him something else and mentioning that it is not what he has lost but perhaps he could play with this for a while. It might not suffice but at least it will show effort until he accepts it is gone.

Drama King?

Q *My four-year-old is so emotional. He responds to everything with high drama. He wants his blue shirt, I give it to him and he wails, 'No the **other** blue one,' like I've just put bamboo shoots under his nails. And you don't want to know the performance he throws if he can't find his blankie . . . Is this just a phase or is he destined for the stage and what can I do about it? I find all the emotion from my little drama king exhausting.*

A Toddlers can be very animated and dramatic. Their highs are very high and their lows are very low. That's part of what makes them so delightful as far as I'm concerned. They are that way because their brains have not yet learnt to regulate their emotions. And guess how they learn how to do it? Through you. It's your response to the situations they're in that teaches them how to behave. When you stay cool and help search for the blankie, when you're calm and help him find the other blue shirt, you are teaching his brain to modulate its response and how to problem-solve. With this kind of support, over time, the drama diminishes.

That being said, some children are more highly emotional by nature than others. This might be true for your child. A child like this is often highly sensitive too.

Regardless of whether this is a passing phase or not, the very best thing you can do when a toddler is highly emotional is to be cool, calm and collected. Don't add to the drama with your own frustration, anger or impatience. That will only make matters worse. Don't label him or put him in a box in your mind or with your words. Don't minimise or make fun of his feelings. Don't punish him for his emotions unless he acts up as a result – hitting, throwing, etc. – and then make it clear you are disciplining him because of that. Simply, calmly help him deal with whatever is causing the upset. And in the heat of the moment, remember that your staying calm is teaching his brain to calm down. And don't forget to enjoy the other side of it – his great joy and happiness and enthusiasm when he's happy! Teaching your child different scenarios and diffusing high emotions early will lead to less emotional meltdowns where he is able to adapt to change more fluidly.

The 'Shy' One

Q *I have twin daughters who are three years old. They truly do complement one another. They are both so very different, but one of my girls has been labelled by my partner as the 'shy' one. It's almost like she is playing on that now and is refusing to eat foods that she would have normally. How do I stop this?*

A I think your instincts are good! Twins, triplets, multiples may be born only minutes or seconds apart, but they all have different little souls and spirits. My take on it is that your daughter, the one labelled the 'shy' one, is probably just a bit more cautious and likes to stand back and watch a little before getting involved. It's amazing how many parents mistake that for being shy. This is a trait I believe we do not want to discourage in our children. It's important that our children are cautious. They are learning naturally from their surroundings whom they can trust. But there is a balance between how you bring your child out of her shell each day and a child playing on that. In this case, there is probably a little bit of that going on at dinner time. I suggest you read the information that I have provided in the eating chapter of this book and then continue to work on her social skills with her sibling when they are playing dress-up. You can easily get involved by creating mini-worlds. This is where you imitate going to the doctor's, or going to the shops. You say things like, 'Good morning, pleased to meet you.' And in return, they give you a response. This will give her a chance to get more familiar with common social situations.

Born Angry?

Q *My daughter has been angry since she came out! She just has a shorter temper than her elder sister and I do think that the family is a little afraid of her. She is a delight when she's getting everything her own way, but terrible if not. How do we head off this behaviour? I feel it's her personality and there may be nothing I can do.*

A I beg to differ that your daughter came out angry! She is just different from her elder sister. Her sister is probably more passive, more obedient, probably more able to adapt to change, whereas you have exactly the opposite with the younger sister, who is more aggressive and alpha. You said the family is a bit afraid of her, which tells me that the rest of you are more like the older sister as well. Because if you were strong-willed like this daughter, you wouldn't be afraid. So when she doesn't get her way, she has a tantrum, which feels to the rest of you like the the Hulk erupting. Now she's learnt to use your fear as leverage to get her own way.

That doesn't mean there is nothing you can do. There is everything that you can do. First you have to understand that she does have a different personality. You need to put boundaries in place, set up expectations, and when the tantrums come, deal with them as I suggest on pages 90–91. Otherwise she will continue to manipulate you all through her behaviour. When she sees it doesn't get her what she wants, the tantrums will diminish.

13

Time Off

All parents need a break; however, for parents of toddlers, that need can be extremely strong as so much of your time can be taken up dealing with limit-pushing, meltdowns and the like. It's easy to feel drained and lose your resilience if you don't have any time off. Time to do nothing except stretch out in the bath or read a book. Time to connect with friends and let your hair down. Time to let go of your responsibilities to your family and remember that you are your own person too so that you can come back to parenting with your batteries recharged. Whether you are in a couple or are parenting solo, every parent needs time off to de-stress and relax.

Not only does every parent deserve alone time and time with friends, but if you are in a couple, you also need 'us time'. Time to remember why you got together in the first place. Time to reconnect without interruptions. Raising a toddler can be so consuming that it's easy to get caught up in day-to-day life and forget to nurture the relationship that began your family in the first place.

Time off is also good for your young ones. It helps them learn that you go, but you come back. It exposes them to other people. It gives them a Mummy and Daddy who are delighted to be with them because they have had a little break.

Not only do you need 'we' time and 'me' time, but parents of toddlers also want to make sure that each parent is doing his or her fair share. Otherwise that creates resentment that can put a strain on your relationship.

Knowing you need time off and taking it are two separate things. Making it happen raises many questions: How do you get your partner to do his part? How can you get out when resources are limited and there seems to be no one to take the kids? How do you make your going smooth for your toddler, who may be experiencing separation anxiety? How do you find the time and energy to rekindle the spark in your relationship with your partner? And how do you deal with your own feelings about leaving her? My answers in this section all revolve around these issues, helping you to make sure you've got sufficient battery-recharging time so that you can be the very best parent for your child.

IN THIS CHAPTER

◆ **Getting partner to help**

◆ **Stuck in house**

◆ **No social life**

◆ **Getting your sexy back**

◆ **Preparing toddlers for your going away**

◆ **Leaving kids without worrying**

Getting Partner to Help

Q *As a stay-at-home parent with two young children under four, I am worn out by the end of the day. How can I get my husband to help with the kids when he gets home? He says he's tired and just wants to veg out on the couch. When I complain, he says it's my job to deal with the kids.*

A Because you're a stay-at-home parent, it's natural that the majority of the childcare does fall on you. But it's important that both parents spend regular one-on-one time with their children. It's how the bonds between parent and child are created and maintained. Plus you deserve a break as well as he does! Rather than complaining, change your tone of voice and attitude. Anger and resentment are brick walls that you can't drive through, so make sure to pick a time when you are both open to discussion. Sit down and tell him what you need from him. Acknowledge that he has long hours a week and so do you, but it's important that you define your parental roles to support one another. If it helps, while talking write down the days your husband will be willing to help out with the kids' bed-time routine. As I said, it is important for him to be involved with the kids as much as he can. It might be your primary job, as his is to go out and be the bread-winner. But raising your children is both of your commitment. This way each of you is clear on how you can help one another. And, of course, make sure you figure out when he and you can have a little down time too.

Stuck in House

Q *I am a stay-at-home mum who literally stays at home 24/7 with our two-and-a-half-year-old and our one-year-old. I am stuck in the house, day in and day out, unless my husband is home from work and we go to the grocery shop. I don't have my driving licence (working on that) so I can't drive anywhere. I wish I could get just a tiny break once in a while. Sometimes I think I am going crazy because the only contact I get with adults is on the phone and that isn't often. No one ever offers to keep the kids for us to have any time to ourselves, and when we ask, usually my parents are already looking after my niece and my mother-in-law is already minding my sister-in-law's children. I keep telling everyone in my family that I need a break, but no one takes me seriously.*

A I have a number of suggestions for you. First, it seems to me that what you need is to be more proactive with your kids so that you can enjoy having fun with them. Definitely continue your driving lessons, as this will give you more freedom to venture out to different places. It most certainly can be a trying time when your children are so young, and you feel like you've been separated from the adult world, as it's very easy to lose ourselves in the world of gaga.

We all need adult mental stimulation. I would suggest talking with your husband to arrange a date night, where you get out, see a film, grab something to eat; or even entertaining at home yourself would be a great starting point. Going to local activities on a weekly basis through clubs or church will give you the opportunity to meet other parents. Arrange coffee mornings, where kids and parents come round to you. You don't seem to mention your friends, where are they? Arrange to go out together when your husband can babysit for the night. Rather than wishing your family members would help out, I would also invest in a reliable, experienced babysitter. And if you cannot afford that, book in your date nights so that you can give your family members plenty of notice so they are available to help.

Balance is important; only you can make time for you because if you don't, nobody else will. A mother who is able to give herself what she needs to feed her own individuality is a mother who is able to give her kids what they need from her. And that's a good place to be!

No Social Life

Q *Our three-and-a-half-year-old daughter kicks up such a fuss if my husband and I try to go out at night that we've given up even trying. Consequently, we have absolutely no social life. I know that's not healthy, but I frankly don't know what to do about it.*

A This is not an uncommon issue and, unfortunately, a lot of parents respond the way you do – taking the path of least resistance and not even trying to turn the situation around. But that is not good for you two – or your child. If she can manipulate you about this, how else is she ruling the roost?

To begin with, you and your husband have to agree that being good parents is not about putting your lives on hold for two decades and that time spent alone outside the home is important to you as a couple to keep the relationship fires burning. That will give you the incentive to push through the drama your daughter is likely to create.

Once you've determined that you will create a social life, here are my tips:

♦ **Don't leave your daughter with someone she's not familiar with. Use a minder she knows well – Grandma or Uncle, perhaps. If you don't have a person like that, have the minder come over a few times during the day while you are at home so she can get comfortable with that person.**

♦ **Plan an evening out – buy tickets to the cinema or a concert, book a table with friends at a restaurant. Having a set thing to do will hopefully make it harder for you to back out.**

♦ **Know what is better for your daughter regarding what time the minder arrives. Some kids do best when the person arrives early so that they can settle into a game before you go out of the door. Other children have worked out that minder arriving means Mummy and Daddy leaving and kick up a ruckus as soon as she appears at the door. In that case, you should be ready to depart immediately. Leave your mobile number with the minder and all relevant emergency numbers too.**

♦ **Don't sneak out; that creates more anxiety. When you are about to go, say that Mummy and Daddy are going out and will be back later. Period. No long explanations of what you're going to do, how you will miss her, how you know she will feel bad but it will be okay. A kiss and cuddle and off you go, no matter what Academy Award performance your daughter is putting on as you close the door.**

♦ **Enjoy your evening. Almost always, the tears will dry before you are even down the drive. Take your mobile with you, but resist the temptation to call and check until later. Know that the babysitter will call you if she needs to.**

Getting Your Sexy Back

Q *I am a young mum of 20, who has 14-month-old triplets. I seem to be doing relatively okay with my kids, largely due to the fact that I have tremendous support from both sides of the family. The problem is my husband and I are both still young and our friends are young without kids. As much as they appreciate we have children, they have been asking us out on special occasions that arise. My husband is up for going to*

these, and insists it is important for us to be doing so. I feel so tired dealing with the kids all day that mustering up the energy is the last thing I want to do. Most of the time I take sleep over sex. All the women in my family say my husband should cut me some slack, but I am scared that this situation could put a wedge between us personally. What is your suggestion?

A Torn on every level – young enough to still go out and enjoy your twenties, but slightly worn at the edges because of the kids. A familiar story. As much as the women in your family empathise with you and say that your partner should just get over it, I do believe it is important to continue feeding your relationship with him. He obviously doesn't want you both to feel that you have lost what you used to have before the kids came along. However, there are slight adjustments that have to take place because now you have your children to consider. It is not impossible to enjoy parenthood and to get out every now and then as well.

First, I would suggest that, when the kids go down for their afternoon nap, you take the opportunity to sleep as well. A 45-minute power nap can make all the difference in the evening. It will allow you time with your partner when your kids go to sleep. On the weekend, give your partner the opportunity to look after the kids for a couple of hours while you rest up so that you have the energy to enjoy an evening out a little bit later than the time you would flake for bed. That will allow you time with your husband while a family members babysits.

As you see, it is possible to have both. You just have to identify what it is stopping you from moving forward and resolve that blip. Besides, getting yourself dressed up, doing your hair, putting on some make-up and a fancy pair of shoes you haven't worn for a long time is a nice way of saying, 'I'm back!'

Preparing Toddlers for Your Going Away

Q *My husband and I have been trying to get away for a break. I've had three babies in four years and we are both exhausted. Our parents have offered to look after them for a week. How do we prepare them for being away from us? I'm so afraid they will hate us or feel abandoned.*

A Hallelujah! Fantastic! How amazing for you both that you have the support of your family to look after your kids for a week. Get booking!

As for preparing your children, what's important is for them to get used to being around their grandparents. Drop them off for an hour or so. Then move from an hour to an afternoon. It's not only good for the kids because it will get them comfortable with being with Grandma and Grandpa, but it's good for the grandparents so they can see what they're getting into. That's the very best thing you can do to prepare your children – and your parents.

When you go away, it's probably easier if the kids are watched at your house because the bedroom's set up and their toys and supplies are there. But if that won't work, just make sure you take a box of toys over to Grandma's and that each child has his familiar little quilt and toys. If they are in nursery or school, they're going to have a structured routine for your parents to follow. If they are at home all day, be sure to go over with the grandparents the kinds of things that they could do with the kids. Keep it pretty simple – all depending on how energetic they are as grandparents.

While you are away, have regular phone calls or Skype before the kids go off to bed, so you get to speak to them and check in with your parents as well. But grab the time off!

Why not?

Worrying when You Leave Your Children

Q *I can never truly relax when I am not with my two children. I am so scared something will happen to them. They are also really anxious when I leave them, but I think that's because they can see how upset I get. Can you give me some techniques for leaving the kids with confidence and not calling or texting the child-minder every ten minutes to check on them?*

A You are experiencing anxiety. In your mind I bet you know the person you've left your children with is more than capable of taking care of them. But it's a control issue: What if something happens and I'm not there. What *if*?

I dealt with this as a nanny when mums used to go back to work. It was not a reflection of their confidence in my ability to do my job. It was them getting used to not being around their kids and learning how to enjoy themselves without them.

I don't think you should fight your anxious feelings. My approach would be to take it slowly. Do just 20 minutes away from them at first, then 40 minutes, then 60, till you work up to going out for an evening. Once you are comfortable with that, work on creating longer times in between calling or texting, knowing that you've left all your contact details with the minder, who will call if something's wrong. So no news is good news. Start with ringing every 30 minutes, then 45, then every hour. Over time you will gain more confidence that things will be all right at home and your anxiety will diminish.

14

Transitions

Transitions, whether they're milestones like your toddler starting nursery or dealing with divorce or everyday small ones like eliminating a dummy or getting used to a child-minder, are all situations that for parents create vulnerability, unpredictability and heightened emotions. And if it's like that for you, imagine what it's like for a toddler.

It's as if we're swimming in the ocean and then a big wave comes. We adults recognise that we have to get on our surfboard and ride the wave. But a child ends up getting hit by the wave. So of course you want to make that wave as painless as possible. Because it can have a huge impact on your little ones when they're so vulnerable and don't have the maturity to understand what's happening. That's what this chapter is about – answering your questions about what will cushion the blow of big transitions like moving, divorce and death in the family for your child.

This chapter also answers parents' most pressing questions about making everyday transitions like weaning from the dummy, getting out of the pushchair, preparing for a new baby or starting nursery easier by putting certain structures, preparation and techniques in place. Easier for your child because you create a sense of security – and easier on you as you move your child on to the next chapter in his life and yours.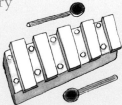

Some of us will find this simple because we may be very organised. For others, it will be more challenging because it will reflect what we need to brush up on to create the necessary structure.

IN THIS CHAPTER

- ◆ Up and out in the morning
- ◆ Getting off the dummy
- ◆ Blankie weaning
- ◆ Introducing child-minder
- ◆ Out of the pushchair
- ◆ Preparing for nursery
- ◆ Not wanting to go to nursery
- ◆ Preparing for a new baby
- ◆ Moving
- ◆ Dealing with divorce and death

Getting out of the Door in the a.m.

Q   *My husband and I both work full-time and our two-and-a-half- and three-and-a-half-year-olds go to a minder. We have such a hard time getting out of the door and into work on time. It's a struggle to get their clothes on and food into their mouths, as well as get ready ourselves. Tantrums are frequent. What can we do to make mornings less chaotic?*

A   This sounds like a simple time-management issue. When both parents work, you absolutely need a schedule and good organisational skills. Start by deciding when you need to be driving away to get to the office on time. Then work backwards to figure out what time you need to get up to be able to get ready without rushing. As you've already experienced, a rushed toddler is a resistant one. Going from one place to another means a transition to a toddler and they need time for those.

Set out clothes the night before as you put your kids to bed, as well as whatever things need to go with them to the minder so you're not scrambling to find things at the last minute. Keep your keys, briefcase, handbag in one place so that you are not running around at the last minute looking for them.

Get up earlier than your kids so you can get ready yourself before focusing on them. Use my Get Up and Go technique to encourage your children to take responsibility in getting ready (see box on page 218). This will help you create a morning ritual so it becomes rudimentary for the kids every day. Morning will become more efficient. Trust me, when this is done successfully you can shave as much as 20 minutes off your get-ready time in the morning. Divide the morning duties between the two of you – one can be making breakfast while the other helps your kids with clothes, teeth-brushing, etc. Use the getting-ready time to give your children some one-on-one attention and the chance to develop life skills like putting clothes and shoes on. Toddler tantrums are often caused not just by being rushed, but because they want to do things for themselves. Make sure you build extra time in for that and hopefully mornings can be transformed from chaos to wonderful times of connection and learning.

GET UP AND GO TECHNIQUE

- ◆ **Make a chart with pictures that show each step your child has to follow – out of bed, wash and dress, eat breakfast, brush teeth – and stick it next to the clock so they will see what they are going to do once they get up.**

- ◆ **In the morning, go into the room and do a pre-wake-up, letting them know it is time to get up: turn on the lamp and gently nudge them awake, reminding them it's time to get out of bed when the alarm goes off.**

- ◆ **When the children get up, have them follow the steps in their routine.**

- ◆ **Give lots of praise and encouragement when they successfully complete a step. The idea is to create as much independence as possible, knowing that, at these ages, they will still need your help in dressing and teeth-brushing.**

Getting Rid of Dummies

My two-and-a-half-year-old is still in love with his dummy. We've tried trading it for toys and such but it hasn't worked. I know I should just take it away but I'm afraid he might become a thumb-sucker if I do. When he doesn't have his dummy, he usually has a thumb or fingers in his mouth. Should I just take the dummy away and then if he sucks his thumb try to solve that later?

When people write to me, I look for key words that jump out and allow me to read between the lines. Your question is very telling, with words like 'We've tried' and 'I know' and 'I'm afraid'. I think what you have to do is make up your mind to get rid of the dummy and just do it. He's old enough now that you can take it away from him, but young enough that he might still go for something else to suck – like his fingers.

Personally, I would stop the dummy because it's not necessary and it can hinder his speech. If he starts putting his fingers in his mouth, you can start to try gently to take them away and tell him not to do it. He's not necessarily going to suck his thumb. But if he does decide to do it, see my advice on thumb-sucking on page 103. Use the Dummy Fairy technique (see box below). It really works *if you allow it to!*

THE DUMMY FAIRY TECHNIQUE

- Tell your toddler, 'The dummy fairy's coming tomorrow to take the dummies!'

- Collect all dummies in your house with your child and place them in a gift bag.

- Hang the bag on a doorknob or place in a sitting area.

- Leave a note for the fairy to take the dummies.

- When he's asleep, throw them in the bin. Make sure they are all gone.

- Leave a small gift inside the bag.

- If possible, sprinkle a few coloured feathers and some glitter around the bag as evidence.

Blankie Weaning

Q *My daughter is three. How do I get her away from that blankie?*

A It's common for toddlers to be attached to an object that comforts and pacifies them. As long as the blankie is not interfering with your daughter's ability to interact with others and play, I personally don't see it as something you have to worry about. Kids grow out of these things on their own, usually by school age. But if you choose to transition her away from it now, try my Blankie Bye Bye technique (see box below). And please make sure that once you have done the technique you also address why she may have needed it.

THE BLANKIE BYE BYE TECHNIQUE

- ◆ **Cut it in half and let her have the half for a few weeks.**

- ◆ **Cut it in half again and let her have that piece for a few weeks.**

- ◆ **When it's a small scrap, announce that the Blankie fairy is coming to retrieve the blankie so that it can be used for all the little baby fairies.**

- ◆ **In the morning, if she looks for it, explain the Blankie fairy retrieved it and that she left a little note and a gift as a thank-you.**

Introducing a Child-Minder

Q *I am about to take that big first-time-parent leap and leave my 14-month-old with a child-minder. Until now, it's been only Grandma and even that was only a few times. What should I do to make this go as smoothly as possible?*

As your baby turns into a toddler, there are many transitions and awarenesses that occur and must be addressed. One big development is the introduction of a new child-minder. Toddlers grasp the fact that 'Mummy and Daddy are leaving', but they don't always understand why they are being left. It's up to you to introduce the minder to your child in advance and to reinforce to your child whenever you leave them that you WILL be returning home to them. This is especially important at your child's age, when separation anxiety can be high. The following guidelines are helpful when it comes to transitioning your child to a child-minder:

- **When hiring the minder for the first time, have her/him over for an hour or two to watch your toddler while you do chores around the house.**

- **Arrange something fun for them to do together, so it's an enjoyable experience. If your child comes to you, take him/her back to the minder and confidently say, 'She/he's here to play with you.' Go back to doing what you were doing.**

- **When the first time you will leave the house arrives, before you go out, make sure you tell your child the minder will be coming. Start with, 'Remember [minder's name] who came to play with you last week? She going to come again tonight while Mummy and Daddy go out.'**

- **Pick out a special activity to do with the minder – a new game or toy, etc.**

- **If you're going out at night, in advance of the minder's arrival, go with your child to his bedroom and together pick out pyjamas for him to wear to bed and a book to read with the minder. Remind him that you will be sure to come in and give a kiss good night when you return. Some children, for reassurance, ask that you wake them up when you return, so they know you're back. I would simply say that he might be fast asleep when Mummy and Daddy get back, but you will see him in the morning.**

- **Don't prolong your leaving. After you brief the minder on dinner time, bed time and routine, kiss your child goodbye, tell him you will be back soon, and leave. The longer you stay in the house while the minder is** there, the more aware your child is that you are leaving and the more time he has to build up anxiety. Be matter-of-fact with your child. You're leaving to go out and you will be back later. Don't feed into his tears or pleas for 'just one more game'.

♦ Know that if your child gets upset or distressed before you leave, that's natural. It may happen the first time or even the first several times you go out. Chances are your anxiety over leaving will last longer than his does!

Getting out of the Pushchair

Q *I've been trying to get my almost-three-year-old to walk home from nursery but he insists on me pushing him in the pushchair. This happens not just to and from school, but everywhere. How can I get him out walking?*

A Parents who do not move their children along in their development disable them slowly. Your son is not encouraged to walk because he doesn't have to. As long as the pushchair is there, he will want to use it. And as long as you give in, the situation will remain the same.

So here is my advice: put the pushchair away for a few days and simply choose to walk with your toddler to places that are near and local. I would advise that you use the Roaming technique before you do this (see page 139). The idea is that you get used to doing short sporadic trips so that he gets used to walking more. Perhaps you walk locally to the park and feed the ducks. Maybe you walk to the post office. Perhaps you are within walking distance of his nursery. The point is he will get used to doing this. Then, when you do take the pushchair out and he asks to sit in it, you can set up the expectation that he can sit in it for ten minutes but then he will have to walk for a while too.

Make sure that when he is walking and you have the pushchair, he is always on the inside of the pavement and holding onto the pushchair or your hand. It has to be one or the other. Always remember road safety. When they start to get a little bit older you will introduce the safety of crossing the road with you, rehearsing what to do and teaching them the signals of when to walk and when to stop so that walking out and about becomes second nature. See the box below for the Green Cross Code, which is the tried and true official British technique for street-crossing.

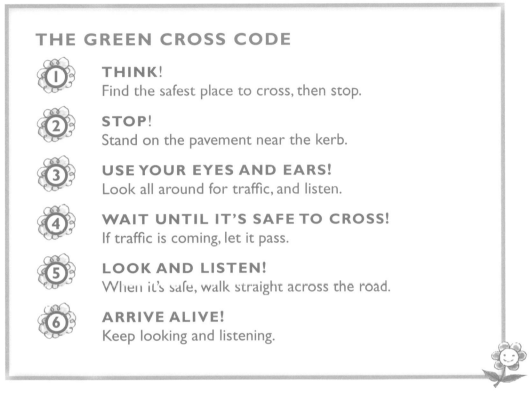

THE GREEN CROSS CODE

1 THINK!
Find the safest place to cross, then stop.

2 STOP!
Stand on the pavement near the kerb.

3 USE YOUR EYES AND EARS!
Look all around for traffic, and listen.

4 WAIT UNTIL IT'S SAFE TO CROSS!
If traffic is coming, let it pass.

5 LOOK AND LISTEN!
When it's safe, walk straight across the road.

6 ARRIVE ALIVE!
Keep looking and listening.

Preparing for Nursery

 My four-year-old starts nursery next month. How do I get him ready for that big first day?

A Going off to nursery is a transition for both of you. For you it marks the end of one stage of parenting and the beginning of another. Most parents feel a lump in the throat as their 'baby' goes off to school for the first time. And as for your child, it's a whole new world with different routines, people and experiences. Some kids take to it easily. Others need more time to settle in. But there are things you can do to make it as smooth as possible:

◆ First, present a calm, confident face to your child about this change so he doesn't pick up on any anxiety on your part. The more you convey this is going to be a fun experience, the more likely it is he'll feel that way too.

◆ Arrange with the nursery for a visit so that he can get a bit familiar with the surroundings in advance. Show him where the coats go, where the bathroom is, what kind of activities go on in each part of the space. Talk to him about all the wonderful things he's going to be doing there.

◆ If you haven't already done so, get your son used to being left with others for periods of time away from the house. Have him go over to a friend's or a family member's house for a couple of hours. That way he will get used to being without you in less familiar surroundings.

◆ Role-play at home being at school. Take turns being the teacher.

◆ Find some good books about the first day of school and read them to him.

◆ Make sure he has a good bed-time routine so that he is well rested. Transitions are harder when a toddler is over-tired.

◆ A week or two before the first day, practise the Get Up and Go technique (see page 218) to get him and you used to getting up and out of the house at a set time. You don't want to be rushing him on that first day.

◆ When the day arrives, give him something of yours, like a scarf, and say, 'Hold on to that for Mummy because Mummy will be back to pick it up.' That can reassure him you will return.

◆ Make your exit quickly. Walk him in, give a kiss and hug, tell him you'll pick him up, and then GO! You are leaving your child in the hands of professionals who will know how to distract him and get him involved in having a positive experience. Your hanging about interferes with that and can stir up more separation anxiety.

Complaining about Going to Nursery

Q *My four-year-old just started nursery and she keeps saying she doesn't want to go. I feel so guilty, but she has to go because I have had to go back to work. Please help me cope!*

A I am sorry you feel so badly. Hang in there! The transition to nursery can be hard on you both, but you can make it easier. Here are my three nursery golden rules to help you and your little one:

1. Persevere

After one or two weeks, you can't just say, 'This isn't working.' You need to give it time for everyone to get used to the new arrangement. Give it a good couple of months for both you and your child. Nothing happens overnight.

2. Arrange Play Dates

Play dates get your little one used to being around other children and sharing toys and activities. They also help your child to settle at nursery. And, it's never too late to help a child settle – no matter how many weeks or months into the schedule they are. Invite children from the nursery to spend time at your house at the weekend, one child at a time. Having a playmate around at nursery will keep her more relaxed and help her to focus on having fun and learning.

3. Go Along for an Afternoon

If you spent an afternoon at nursery with your child when she/he was first settling in, it might help to do it again for the new term, so she/he feels like it's a fresh start. I suggest afternoon rather than morning so that you don't have to make an escape later to go to work, which can upset your daughter. You just arrive earlier than normal for the pick-up.

Preparing for a New Baby

Q *I am pregnant with my second child and would appreciate your ideas on how to create as smooth a transition as possible for my three-year-old.*

A How soon in advance to tell your child is really up to you. Some parents wait till almost the last minute; others let their toddler know months in advance. Either way, of course, you want to talk about it in the most positive way possible – how much fun it will be, how he will get to be a big brother. Involve him in getting ready for the baby's arrival; share the name if you choose. But truthfully, all of this is very abstract to a toddler. The real transition happens when you bring the baby home and big brother has to accept the new reality.

To make that as smooth as possible, my number one suggestion is to keep his routine the same if you can. His routine gives him a great sense of security and stability and he's already dealing with one BIG change. Wait a while to add in potty-training or any other transition. Also, be sure to have regular alone time with him. I know that can be challenging with a newborn, but it will go a long way towards reducing his jealousy. To do that, you may need your partner to step up to the plate more. Don't be afraid to ask for help from him and from relatives and friends. Make sure your toddler has special time with Dad too during the transition.

Another thing that helps a toddler adjust to a new baby is to give him a doll that he can take care of. Have him mimic your actions while you are taking care of the baby. That will help him not to feel left out. And be sure to include him in caring for the baby. He's too young to actually do anything, and he can never be left alone with his sibling, but you can allow him to give you suggestions. Ask, 'Shall we put her in this or that? What song shall we sing?' This will help him feel included. Finally, don't worry overmuch if he expresses negative feelings about the baby. He needs time to adjust. However, do watch for any aggression towards the baby and be sure to teach him to be kind and gentle.

Smooth Moves

Q *We are moving house and my son keeps crying as he sees everything being packed away. Could you give me some advice on how I can settle him in quickly to our new home?*

A This one is simple. As soon as you move into the house, the first thing to do is set up his bedroom. That way he will see the known and the familiar and that will make him feel more secure.

There are also things you can do before moving day. Right now, he's feeling a bit of instability because things are moving around him and there's not much explanation. People are coming and going. Bags are being packed and going out of the door. Talk to him about what is happening: 'We're packing things up because we're going to our new home. We're going to have lots of fun there.' If possible, take him to the new house if you haven't already. Make him feel like part of the process and he will not be as anxious.

Toddlers and Divorce

Q *I split with my son's father. Before then, my 20-month-old son was in a lovely routine, going straight down after a night bottle. Since moving back to my parents' house, my son will not sleep in his cot. He screams and kicks. I've relented and let him sleep with me because of the guilt I feel for splitting up the family. I usually now lie with him for an hour at night trying to get him to sleep. I don't know how to get him back into his routine. I keep thinking I should wait until I'm settled in our own house, otherwise another move is going to upset him again.*

A You are going through the second most stressful situation: divorce. The impact is taking its toll on the two of you, and I understand how a disruption in your son's environment and how everybody is feeling emotionally could lead to his sleeping in your bed.

However, an hour to get him to sleep is not working. How long is it going to take until you are in your own home? If it's two weeks I would wait until then. But if it is going to take longer than a month, I suggest you create a bed-time routine right now. Once you have consistency with the bed-time routine where you are able to create more of a ritual and a calm sleeping environment, then it's time to embrace the Sleep Separation technique (page 185). You have to remember the family dynamic has changed and there is a lot of unsettlement for the pair of you. Your son senses your hurt. Also he is used to having his father around and is trying to adapt to his new environment. His kicking and screaming is an emotional meltdown and not from defiance. For whatever the reason, this is your new situation, so embrace the love and support you have around you and create the stability your son needs.

Explaining Death to a Toddler

 How do you explain death, funerals, burying people to a toddler? We just had a death in the family.

A I'm so sorry for your loss. The most important thing for parents to understand is that, whether it's a family member who has passed away or a pet that has had to be put to sleep, toddlers experience a loss when someone they have had a relationship with dies, just like we adults.

When toddlers are very young they simply do not understand the concept of finality. It's like the person they don't see any more has gone on a long vacation. Children will choose different times and days out of the blue to bring up questions regarding where that person is now. Those with strong religious beliefs hold on to much faith and visually create a picture of where their beloveds are. Older children experience sadness and loss but can move straight away on to something that makes them roll into laughter.

The fact is, there is no wrong or right way of dealing with bereavement. Each one of us uniquely has our own journey. I generally think it is always good to allow your children the chance to talk fondly of their memories and experiences shared. If it helps, you can collect a chest full of photos and items that capture those moments. Leave it freely open for whenever your older toddlers want to visit it.

Acting up after Death in Family

Q *My mother recently passed away suddenly and my three-and-a-half-year-old's previously occasional temper tantrums are now daily and have become explosive. My mother was a huge part of our daily lives and was our daycare for the first year of our daughter's life as well as our primary care backup. I don't know how much children this age understand about death but she seems to understand she's gone.*

Prior to this tragedy, we weren't very successful in any form of discipline as everything we tried just seemed to make things worse. We live in a block of flats with neighbours on both sides and not very much insulation in between. My daughter will scream at the top of her lungs – high-pitched, blood-curdling screams. We cannot stop her. Nothing seems to work.

A First, my condolences. It is incredibly difficult for a family to deal emotionally with the loss of a loved one and it's even more of an impact when we are dealing with shock from sudden death. Trust me, I know from my own experiences. No doubt the fact that your mother was a huge part of your life means a void now for both you and your daughter.

Your daughter is definitely picking up your feelings, as well as experiencing a sense of loss of her own. Grieving is a process and, right now, any behaviour you are trying to curb will seem highly magnified to your daughter because of the emotional state you are in. However, you may feel like you've lost your mind, but you haven't lost your common sense. The statement you made that you're held to 'ransom by your neighbours' is right, because you have been. That's a choice, my dear. Even death has boundaries and unacceptable behaviour still needs to be addressed. Know the difference between her having an emotional meltdown due to the circumstances and just being a little girl testing the boundaries. It will allow you to identify what behaviour needs to be addressed with the Naughty Step, and what situations need to be talked about.

I would read my answer to the question above yours and also make it clear to your child it's okay to have her feelings about Grandma and to talk to you about them. Because if she sees you upset it might make her feel like she cannot mention Grandma. When you do feel sad you can say to her, 'Mummy feels sad, because Grandma is not here with us.' If she asks you where she has gone, you can choose to deal with it the way you want to.

It's also important that you continue to nurture and be kind to yourself through this difficult time. I'd like to recommend a book to help you out. It's called *On Grief and Grieving,* by Elizabeth Kübler-Ross and David Kessler. I hope it will bring you some sanity and peace of mind whilst finding the strength at this most difficult time.

Afterword

I said at the beginning of this book that it takes patience, perseverance, follow-through, consistency and repetition to raise a toddler. What's most important for you is to recognise what allows you to have *more* of those five factors in order to resolve the questions you have during these years. If you are a very smart parent, you wouldn't have just gone to the parts that were relevant to you right now. You would have read the whole of this book and seen some of the other issues that parents are having so that you can better understand how to avoid being in a similar place.

I hope reading this book has confirmed for you that you're not going through a particular problem on your own, because there are millions of people worldwide experiencing the same issue. Even though you may be reading a question unique to a specific family, there are fundamental challenges that every family has with toddlers which reflect the stages they are going through, whether that regards behaviour, sleeping, eating, getting along well with others or being out in public. The more I can educate you as a parent in understanding the way your toddler thinks, behaves and interprets what you say, the closer you become to her. And the closer you become to her, the more insight you have into how she thinks. That makes the journey more enjoyable for you. I also hope you now understand that how you respond makes the difference in resolving your challenge quickly or more painfully. You decide!

Your problem can feel so huge when you're alone dealing with it. That's why, while I continue to help families on TV shows and books, I also want to encourage you to reach out to me on Twitter at https://twitter.com/jo_frost and via my website at www.jofrost.com. You can not only connect to me but also reach out to other parents and talk about those issues so that we can all help each other.

That's really all I could ask for – to be able to give my knowledge and expertise as a woman who has dedicated herself to this parental arena and hope that you will take all of it to the best of your ability and be happy with who you are as a parent today and feel encouraged to be an even better parent tomorrow. And then spread what you've learnt!

Fondly,

Jo
x

Index

A

B

D

quality time 4, 9–10, 13, 109

Y